EXT SU_ANNE:
A STORY OF RESURRECTION AND REDEMPTION

SUZANNE JACOBS

outskirts
press

TABLE OF CONTENTS

It all started in Iowa. The good and the bad memories. The events that began the downward spiral of my life began here in a Victorian style three story house with a huge fenced in backyard and two staircases, one of which was spiral. It was located in a great family-oriented neighborhood. We knew all of our neighbors and would frequently get together with them for various occasions. They would watch my brother and I and we would watch their dogs and water their plants when they were out of town. All of our neighbors were so fun to be around especially around the holidays. They would always go all out for the holidays especially Halloween and Christmas. Every year they would transform their yards and houses into a haunted scene for Halloween or a Christmas wonderland. We were all great friends and they were all people I loved dearly.

My three closest friends were only a matter of a few blocks away. Haley lived just a block away which meant we spent a lot of time at each other's houses. I remember her house was always crazy and busy because she had seven other siblings. They all looked after us in their own ways and made us into their little Barbie dolls on occasion. Zach lived two blocks away in a civil war headquarters house. His house was filled with secret passages which meant it was the best house for hide and seek. We all spent hours exploring those passages. Andrew lived three blocks away in what I imagined a mansion would look like. It was built up on a hill that overlooked the Mississippi River. He had a wide grand staircase that circled down into the main lobby. His room was bigger than the entire upstairs of my house combined. We would spend hours playing with his various train sets and nutcrackers. When we weren't inside playing, we were outside playing with his many rabbits. He always said he wanted to be a Veterinarian when he grew up and I had no doubt in my mind that he would.

Frequently us four would get together and spend the days outside playing either at a park or in someone's backyard. We were the best of friends and nobody could split us apart. At school we were all in the same class which I'm sure caused headaches for the all the teachers since we were always getting in trouble for talking or goofing off. We couldn't wait to spend more and more time with each other. My friends all loved my parents just as much as I did and I loved their parents just as much as they did. We were definitely a group that could not be split up and you could always count on us to go where the other was going.

My father at this time worked at the local newspaper as an editor. I didn't really know what this meant, but I loved visiting him while he was there. My favorite place in the whole building was the dark room where they made the pictures. There was something cool in this room that was like no other room I had ever been in. It was dark, but light at the same time. It was like magic watching the pictures appear on the pages. I was mesmerized and could have spent hours in that room watching the magic. There were times when he would wait to develop the pictures until I was there to watch it and see the excitement that came over my face.

My father to me looked as if he were a giant as he stood proudly at six feet two inches. He was tall, lean, and a strong man with dark, black hair. His eyes were also dark, but welcoming. He had a sense of warmth and care about him. My mother was of average height measuring at five feet five inches tall. Unlike my father though, she was a little over the average weight. Her hair was a beautiful brown that she curled under every morning with soft, gentle, and welcoming blue eyes. She was sweet, gentle, kind, and caring. She loved my brother and me with all of her being and told us on many occasions that she loved us. My parents were the typical hard-working middle-class type of folks. They worked hard for everything they got and didn't take anything for granted. They loved my brother and me very much and would spend time with us. On many occasions we would play some type of sport in our yard or catch fireflies in the summers. In the winters we would all go sledding together and have snowball fights. They provided my brother and myself with what we needed and with their love.

My mother at this time quit her job to raise my brother and myself. I remember on many occasions baking cookies with her and helping out around the house. I always felt like I was big stuff when I was getting to vacuum with my mother or mow the lawn with my father. My brother and I spent more time playing outside in the warm sunshine than watching TV. We would climb the trees and run wild and free without a care in the world. During this time she often took us out for daytrips which usually included the park, the library, and the river. My favorite place was down by the river surrounded by shaded trees. Down there I would curl up under one of the trees and watch the river flow by as I listened to it lapping against the banks. I would make shapes out of the clouds and listen to the birds as they flew by. Sometimes I would take a book down there, but mostly I just went to be alone and to truly feel safe. This was where I always felt the happiest and the most at ease. I didn't have a care in the world while I was there listening to the river and birds, feeling the sunshine on my face, and looking up at the clouds. I never had anything to fear while I was there; I was truly at ease by the river. The river became my refuge and my protector as the years went by. It was there that I could think. It was there where I could be safe. It was there where I could be me.

During Halloween we would get two big pumpkins and two small pumpkins. My brother and my father would always make the jack-o-lanterns while my mother and I painted the small pumpkins. When it came time to pick out a costume, we would always look for things around the house. We didn't have much extra money so we made do with what we had. I can remember going as a clown one year, a Dalmatian whose spots fell off and turned into looking like a mouse, and an umpire one year when I put on my father's gear. With our buckets in hand we walked all over town it seemed like until our buckets were overflowing with all sorts of shapes and sizes and colors of candy packages.

The day after Thanksgiving we would put up the Christmas tree and all of the decorations. We would watch Christmas movies and sing Christmas songs all day long. Every year my parents would take us to the mall to make cookies and a new ornament or two to hang on the tree while they walked around and judged wreaths and trees. By the time they picked us up to go back home I had eaten about ten cookies and made two or three new ornaments. I always went to bed that night with a belly ache, but before I could go to bed we had to put our new ornaments on the tree. This meant that the decorations were complete. My favorite part of the tree was lying under it and watching the lights change. I was just as mesmerized with this as I was with the dark room. Christmas day was not anything that special to me. What was special to me were the events leading up to the day.

I always thought that I had a great family until one fateful day. It was a day that I could never forget. A day that has been the root of it all. A day that changed my life forever.

My brother and I were playing and got into a fight. I wanted to play with his toys and he didn't want me to play with them. We started getting louder and louder until I decided that I was going to go tell on him for not sharing. I ran downstairs with my brother on my heels to go tell my father what was going on. I was yelling as loud as I could so he could hear me over my brother. My father turned around and yelled at both of us to stop. I stopped and then took the silence as an opportunity to get out my side of the story. This only made my father mad and told us both to get upstairs. We both stomped up the stairs with our father on our tails. I turned the corner and leaned against a piece of wall no wider than a foot. Firmly my father asked what was going on and who started it. My brother and I both began to talk at the same time which didn't settle well with my father. Then it happened. My father turned, looked at me, made a fist, pulled his arm back and punched me in the face. Luckily I ducked, but when I looked up his hand was in the wall. I ran into my room and hid underneath my bed. I put all of my stuffed animals in between me and the wall thinking they would protect me. I didn't come out for the rest of the day and slept there that night. My father never even came in to check on me and neither did my mother. They never called for me to come to dinner or anything. They stayed downstairs as I hid under my bed.

MY BROTHER

MY BROTHER WAS so excited when my parents told him he was going to be a big brother that he kept telling everyone he was going to be a big brother to a little sister. He never talked about having a brother, only about having a sister, so much so that he went and bought me a pink dress before I was born. He couldn't have been happier when I was born and to see me in that dress he picked out. My brother was always eager to help my parents and to feed me. He truly loved me and wanted the best for me.

My brother is five years older than me so I relied on him for everything. He was my protector and best friend and the guy I ran to for everything first. His true protective colors came out when I started school. He would walk me home every day and check on me throughout the day at school. If anyone even thought of bullying me, he was right there to stop it and stick up for me. He had decided that he was the only one that could bully me and everyone else would have to go through him first.

I loved my brother with everything I had and always wanted to play with him. We would make up some of the best games and get into so much trouble together. He showed me some of the best hiding spots and how to correctly shoot a Nerf gun. No matter what the circumstances were, I felt safe around him. I didn't think he could do any harm or hurt anything in the world. I even felt safe when he took my clothes off. I don't know why I felt safe when he did that, but because I was so young, I guess I didn't really know any better. What does a three-year-old know about those types of things? I didn't even know boys and girls had different parts. That is until my brother pointed it out.

When he would undress me while my parents thought we were playing with Transformers and Gi-Joe's I thought it was normal. I thought that everybody did this. I didn't think anything was wrong especially since my brother told me to do it. He would tell me it was time to "have fun." He would take off all of my clothes and then he would take his off. He would rub me up and down my body and then make me rub him in the same way. He would then tell me to rub his penis and to make him happy.

As I grew older and older things changed. He started making me take my clothes off while he watched then just staring at me and he started becoming violent with his requests. He told me that if I didn't "make him happy" then he would spank me with either his belt or a wooden spoon that he kept in his room. I never thought my brother, the guy I loved to spend time with, my protector, my friend would ever do anything to hurt me, but I quickly realized he was not my protector anymore. I became afraid of him and didn't want to ever see him. I didn't want to be anywhere near him, but my parents made us play together. I dreaded these times and wished for them to stop. He was becoming something I never wanted to be around and started to hit me for no apparent reason.

These times of "having fun" as he would call it would be a time of torture, fear, and pain. It all began to start the same way. He would make me undress for him while he watched and stared as tears welled up in my eyes. Then I would have to get on my knees as the tears streamed down in my face and he would take his pants off. He would then stand in front of me and force his penis in my mouth while I tried not to gag and choke on tears; all the while he was holding that wooden spoon of his. After he was satisfied with this he would tell me to get on the bed, but if he was not satisfied he started hitting me with the spoon wherever he wanted to. Once we were on his bed he would get on all fours and look down at me. He would do whatever he wanted to do until he was ready and he would penetrate me time after time after time. I cried and begged and pleaded for him to stop, but it was of no use. He didn't care as long as he was getting what he wanted. My cries and pleas were useless. It was like he turned a blind ear and eye to me. He only cared about what he wanted and nothing else. That love I used to have for him was now gone and that sense of protection he once had was now nonexistent. I knew by this point that this was wrong. That this wasn't normal. That this had to stop somehow. I also knew that I wanted nothing to do with my brother. I never wanted to be around him again. He became a nightmare living in the room next to mine. He became something I hated and something I was scared of.

MOVING TO FULTON

AT THE END of my third grade year my family decided to move to Fulton, Missouri. I thought that with this change everything in my life would change and my nightmare would end. I was devastated to leave my friends that I had such a strong bond with. We were inseparable for so many years; I thought this move would destroy that. My friends were the world to me. They helped me cope with everything going on behind closed doors even though they didn't know about any of it. They were the shining lights in my dark world and I couldn't imagine leaving them. All we knew was that we were going to write letters back and forth and try to stay just as close, but I was still far from excited about this move. I would be leaving my bright shining happy lights and the river as my refuge behind. How would I ever make such good friends again and where could I run to and hide now?

I decided that if I ignored the inevitable then maybe it wouldn't actually happen. Maybe I wouldn't have to actually move away from my friends and the people I loved dearly. Maybe I wouldn't have to leave my secret place of comfort. I went through the summer playing with my friends and pretending to not see the piles of boxes get bigger and bigger. I avoided packing at all costs and didn't want to be anywhere near my house. With each day, the inevitable was getting closer and closer and becoming clearer and clearer that it was going to happen. It finally came to a point where I couldn't ignore it anymore and had to say goodbye to my friends. Saying goodbye absolutely broke my heart and theirs. After saying goodbye I didn't know what to do. All I felt was complete sadness knowing that I would not ever see them again.

While we were driving to Fulton I began to think that with this move things were going to change. That maybe moving would change my brother and shake him up as much as it had shook me up. That just maybe he would stop and everything would go back to being okay. We would go back to being a family that cares about one another and my brother would become my best friend and protector again. Instead of hurting me he would realize what he has been doing and would stop it.

When we moved there my mother decided that she needed to get a job to help with the ever growing expenses. This meant that both of my parents would be spending more time at their jobs and less time at the house. It quickly became apparent that this was not a good equation to my problem. My wishes and hopes of my brother stopping this abuse stayed as just that….wishes and hopes. With both of them being gone more often and for longer periods of times this allowed my brother the extra time he apparently needed now. This extra time only intensified everything and made my nightmare that much worse. He became much more violent when he wanted to "have fun." Instead of the abuse lasting 15 or 20 minutes as it had before it now would last for at least an hour and usually longer. I became terrified to come home after school knowing that he would be there waiting for me. I wished for school to last longer and tried to get involved in as many activities as I possibly could. I wanted to do anything besides going home to him. He soon lost his name in my mind and became a cruel and evil fiend. A daily terror that I couldn't get away from no matter how hard I tried.

Things only continued to escalate and get worse while I grew closer to my breaking point. I couldn't take this anymore and something had to happen. I thought that maybe if I fought back just once things would get better. I was older and stronger by now and maybe he would take my pleas seriously this time. I didn't really have a plan as to what I was going to do, I just knew that I had to do something.

It was a Thursday when I finally found the courage to fight back in a different way. He took me downstairs to the back of the basement where we had a tan and off-white gingham couch, a recliner, a TV and a good collection of VHS movies. He had already pulled the bed out of the couch and rearranged the furniture so that it would fit. He also had recently changed from having a wooden spoon to having a ping pong paddle and it was already in there on the TV stand. As I scanned the room I was fighting to find that courage I felt before I walked in the house and saw him. I knew exactly what his next statement was going to be, but it still sent chills through me every time he said it. Every time I couldn't believe that he was saying it again and that this was happening again. I had lost count so very long ago of how many times he had made that statement, but it still surprised me to hear him say those four words. "Take off your clothes." he ordered. I stood there as my adrenaline accelerated, my palms were sweating, my breathing quickened, and my heart beat faster and faster with each small breath. *This is the moment to find that courage. This has to stop and I have to stop it somehow. The time is now!* "I'm not going to take my clothes off this time!" I said in a shaky voice. Gaining my confidence I said it again, but this time with a stronger voice. I was determined that this abuse was going to end. My brother turned and looked at me with his eyebrows raised and said in a low raspy voice, "You will take your clothes off!" "This is wrong and it can't happen anymore." I said in response, losing a little bit of that confidence and courage. "This isn't wrong! You don't know what you're talking about. You're only eight years old. How could you know that this is wrong? If I tell you to do something you do it.

Now do as I said and take your clothes off!" He said in a harsh voice and I could see his blood begin to boil. With the last ray of hope and courage I said, "But, you are my brother. You're supposed to protect me, not hurt me, and this is wrong." I became very frightened when he charged me, grabbed me by my arms and threw me down. *What do I do now? He won't listen to me!* As I was down on the ground he stood over me and screamed with a red face "You take your clothes off now!" Even though I was trembling in fear, I was determined that this was going to end tonight and I wasn't going to take my clothes off. I prayed in those few seconds that God would protect me and that this would stop. But before I could finish praying, he was tearing my clothes off of me. I tried with all the strength I had to keep my clothes on, but he was too strong and all my trying failed in the end. In just a few short seconds I was laying there on the ground, crying, and naked with this guy who was supposed to be my brother looming over me. "Stop all of that ridiculous crying and be a good girl and do as I tell you!" he shouted at me. *I don't want to do what you tell me to do, this isn't right, I can't do this anymore. I can't do this, I won't do this, he's my brother, and this isn't supposed t....* My thoughts were interrupted when he slapped me across my face and then turned me over and started to spank me. "Stop this!" I choked out between my tears and screams. But he didn't stop, he only spanked me harder as he smiled because of the pain he was causing me. Every hit sent a chill through my body and just when I thought I couldn't take anymore, he told me to start counting every hit. "Please.....stop.....this, please... please! It was barely audible, but loud enough for him to hear it. "I said to start counting and don't you mess up!" he said in a cold voice. With the next hit, I reluctantly said "one." "You count louder or you're going to get it worse! Do I make myself clear bitch?!" "Yes." I said in a crushed voice. "We're starting over and this time it's going to be harder!" *I have to say it louder? How much louder does he want it? I am in so much pain, I can't take this....* Right then his hand comes swinging down and I say in a loud, clear voice, "One." I try my best to say the numbers in a loud, clear voice, but once we got to 15, it was hard to understand what number I was saying. *Come on Suzanne, just get through this and maybe it'll all be over. Say them loud and clear or it's all going to start over! Here it comes...* "16" I said through the sobs. This continued in the same manner until we got to number 30. *Thank God it's over!* Right as I think that, he pulls me back by my hair and says in a low, deep, cold voice "Don't you ever say no to me again and disrespect me like that! Do you understand me you filthy bitch?" "Yeah I understand." "Now apologize to me!" "I'm sorry." I replied in a defeated voice. "Damn right you're sorry, but what are you sorry for?" "I'm sorry for saying no to you and for disrespecting you." I said in a subjugated voice. "That's more like it! Now you're really going to apologize by giving me exactly what I want...right you no good bitch?!" *No I'm not! No I can't!* "Yes." *Why did you say that Suzanne? You're so stupid! This was supposed to end tonight, now when will it end?* "Good now turn over!" he said with the biggest smile on his face and a twinkle in those cold, cold eyes. As I turned over, he pulled his pants down to expose himself. As he scooted up toward my face, he rubbed himself all over me. "Open your mouth, and don't you dare bite or you'll really get it!" *Just don't open your mouth. It's not that hard, just keep it closed. This will work!* Just as I was feeling confident about my plan, he pinched my nose close and then I had to open my mouth and for the second my mouth was open, he pushed his penis in my mouth. I tried to push him off as I screamed. He just held my arms down as tears were streaming down my face. "Suck it NOW!" I shook my head no, but that only made him more furious so he took his penis out of my mouth and turned me over once again, but this time he used a paddle. He spanked me harder than I had ever been spanked. He spanked me for what seemed like an eternity and then turned me over and said, "Are you going to suck it now?" "Yes." I said as I felt so ashamed for not ending this tonight, but only making things worse. Once again he shoved his penis in my mouth and held down my arms. *What else can I do? He is going to get what he wants one way or another. There's no way that I can stop him. He's too strong and I'm too weak. He can throw me around like a ragdoll and I can't do anything about it. When will this ever stop?* Tears were coursing down my face and all I wanted was for him to take it out of my mouth. *I have already gagged three times. How many more times am I going to gag? God, please just make this stop! Make him stop this! This can't still be going on. Please just make him stop this.* My prayer was answered but only for him to move down my body. With every last ounce of strength I had I tried to clamp my legs shut but he easily over-powered me and stuck his penis in me as far as he could. *God, Please stop this! Please make this be a bad dream instead of my life! Please stop this! God this hurts so bad! Why is he doing this to me? Why does he think he can do this? I am his sister. This isn't supposed to be happening! This isn't supposed to be happening. Not now. Not ever. God, please make this go away. I can't handle this pain any longer, but he's too strong for me to do anything.* After what seemed like an endless amount of time, he finally stopped. When he had finished he just stared at me for a perpetually long amount of time and at last told me to get dressed. "Never, ever disrespect me like that again bitch or you will get it worse next time! Now get upstairs! I don't want to hear you or see you!" he said in an uncompromising voice.

I ran upstairs to the bathroom as fast as my little eight-year-old legs would allow me to and my blurry vision would let me. This was the only room I could go to that had a lock on it and every day I took full advantage of it. I quickly got in the shower to wash Him off of me. I felt so dirty on so many levels. I just wished water would wash it all away. The scars, the memories, the nightmares, the sounds, the pain, and the fear. I longed to be a normal kid like all the ones in class with me. To have a brother that truly cares about me. To have a family that loved me. As I tried to calm down I thought of my spot in Iowa under the shade tree with the river rushing, the birds singing, and the sun shining on my face. I tried to think of my friends in Iowa that were an ever present joy in my life where now there seems to be no joy.

After my disappointing shower I quickly grabbed my basketball and snuck out of the house. I went down to the basketball goal about a block away. I knew I would at least be alone here and I wouldn't have to hear Him do anything. I tried to play basketball, but I was in too much pain. It was a feat in just walking down here much less doing anything else. I had to get away from that house and away from Him. I didn't want to be there if he got a second wind. I just wanted to be alone and the second I was the tears gushed down my face onto the pavement. I was once again a failure. I tried to stop it but couldn't. I gave into the pain and the fear like always. How would this ever stop with how big of a coward I was being? How would this ever stop?

Days turned into weeks and weeks turned into months and nothing changed. I had lost all hope and will to fight. I just did as he told me to and prayed that it wouldn't last long. My will was completely crushed and I was completely devastated. I became desolate and didn't have any joy or happiness in my life. I knew what every day had in store for me and with each passing day it became harder and harder to get out of bed.

TURN OF EVENTS

IN THE SUMMER between my fourth and fifth grade year my brute of a brother made a lot of friends that he spent more and more time with. He went from abusing me every day, to every other day, to a couple times a week, to once a month, to none at all. As thankful as I was for this change I was always looking for the time that he would start back up. I was continually fearful of him and never wanted to be around him. When my fifth-grade year started the abuse had died down drastically. During this school year he got more involved in school activities and we didn't have as much time by ourselves. I was so very thankful for this but was ever ready for him to start back up. When I came home from school he was not there waiting for me as he had previously done for so long. This was quite the shock to my system and I didn't know what to do or think about it.

With this change of events I slowly began to find some hope. I started to notice things that once made me happy and I started to talk to people. I was able to make some friends at school and for once I felt like I was a normal kid. I didn't feel like I was living a nightmare anymore. I was becoming more and more comfortable and confident that my brother wasn't going to abuse me anymore. I began playing basketball with neighbors and laughing and smiling once again. I started listening to music again and playing the piano. I started to find joy when I thought I wouldn't ever experience that again.

The Counselor

It was October of my fifth-grade year when I was called into the school counselors' office. I had only been in there one other time. In his office he had a desk that faced one of the two windows with two chairs in front of it. Beside the two chairs to the right there was a large gray filing cabinet and beside his desk were two more filing cabinets. His office was not decorated in any sort of way and it was not that big when compared to the other offices in the school. There wasn't anything spectacular about it. He didn't have any pictures or inspirational sayings. He had a small neatly piled stack of papers on his desk and that was it besides his name plate. It was a plain office with nothing inviting about it.

I didn't know why I was being called in there, but I also didn't really question the reason. When I got there I noticed that his blinds were shut and thought that was a little out of the ordinary, but once again I didn't question it. What I did find extremely odd was the fact that he sat beside me instead of at his desk. I thought why would he be sitting beside me and wondered if I had done something wrong. What happened next made me wish I had questioned being called down there and why his blinds were closed. It made my heart stop and my mind to panic when he put his big burly hand on my thigh. I learned long ago with my brother that when he put his hand on my thigh, he was going to strip me down and have his way with me. I couldn't believe this was going to happen.

I have to do something; I have to get out of here somehow. Think Suzanne, think! "I have to get back to class because we're working on a project" I said. *That should do the trick. He can't keep me in here when I have schoolwork to do.* "Your class is out to recess by now" he said. I quickly glanced to look at the clock and sure enough my class was at recess. *What am I going to do now? Think of something else, anything else and quickly!* "Well I really need to get back to my class and make sure that I didn't miss anything and then get out to recess." I started to walk towards the door and I thought that I had convinced him. Just as I was reaching out to turn the doorknob, he grabbed the back of my shirt and pulled me towards him. *What am I supposed to do now?* He then threw me into the corner between the chairs and the wall with such force that I hit my head and before I could even put my hand on the back of my head he was standing over me. He then got down on his knees and began to pull down my pants. *Why is this happening???* *This can't be happening again!!! Why didn't he just let me go? Doesn't he know this is wrong....or am I the one that is wrong since both him and my brother have done this? He can't be doing this though! There's no way that this can be right! How do I get out of this? How do I make it stop???* I squirmed and squealed and hit him until he slapped my legs and told me to shut up. There wasn't anyway that I was going to stop. I kept squirming, hitting, scratching, and screaming, but it didn't seem to faze him. It only seemed to make him more determined and after a few more blows to my legs he was finally able to pull down my pants and underwear. I was so embarrassed and tried with all my might to pull my pants back up, but my efforts were useless. My screams quickly became worthless when he clamped his hand over my mouth with such force that I couldn't move my head. He then climbed on top of me and pulled his pants down. *This can't be happening! I can't move, I can't stop it! Should I just give in and let him have his way. I can't scream or kick or anything! God, please make this stop, PLEASE STOP THIS!!* He then made sure I knew exactly what he was going to do to me. By this time I was crying uncontrollably and it was getting harder and harder to breathe. He put his penis right in my face to make sure that I saw it and then he moved back down and penetrated me. I screamed out and cried even harder because of the pain. *Oh God please make this stop! I can't handle this! This pain is too much! Make this go away. Make him go away. Let somebody hear my screams and my cries! Please help me! Help me! This has to stop it hurts too bad! Oh God it hurts…it hurts too much.. How much longer is this going to go on? Oh God please make it stop. Make him stop….Please make him stop.* He kept taking it in and out as I laid there useless, not able to do a thing. After an immeasurable, fearful, tearful, painful amount of time he finally eased up on his pressure and was finally finished. *Oh thank you God. He finally stopped…finally. I feel like my insides have been ripped out, but he finally stopped.* He then stood up and put his pants back on and told me to get dressed as if nothing had just happened. He then looked me square in my eyes and said in a demanding voice, "If you ever tell anyone, you will get it much worse next time." He then wiped my eyes and had me blow my nose and sent me on my way back to class. Right before I turned the doorknob he said "You be a good girl now" in an icy voice that sent shivers down my spine.

I walked hunched over holding my stomach as fast as I could to my classroom as the tears coursed down my face. My teacher, Mrs. Williams was sitting at her desk when I walked in. "Everyone is outside at recess. Grab your coat and run on out there." she said. I didn't want to be outside, at school, or at home. I didn't belong anywhere and I couldn't get away from anything anymore. School had become my refuge over the past year. At least while I was at school I was safe….safe until now. I walked over to my desk and sat down defeated. I couldn't stop the tears that were now creating a puddle on my desk and I couldn't believe the sounds I was making through the sobs. Mrs. Williams quickly came over to me and wrapped her arms around me. In those few moments I remembered what it was like for someone to love me. For someone to care about me. For someone to hug me. "Suzanne, what's wrong? What happened?" she asked in a worried voice. I couldn't answer her. I couldn't do anything but sit there and cry as she held me. I felt like my body had been ripped open and wouldn't ever go back together again, but I also felt loved by my teacher and I didn't want that to go away. I didn't want to tell her because she may not love me anymore just like everyone else. "Suzanne, you have to tell me what's wrong. Everything will be okay. You just have to tell me." she said. *He said if I told I would get it worse. How could it get worse? What could have been worse than today? He told me not to tell. He told me it would get worse....it would get worse....then what do I do? Everything won't be okay though. Nothing has been okay. Nothing has!* "What happened at the counselor's office?" she asked me. "I can't tell you." I said through the cries. "Suzanne, you can tell me anything." she said in a soft and gentle voice. "He told me I couldn't tell anyone." I replied. "You can tell me. Suzanne everything will be okay. I'm right here and I'm not going anywhere. Tell me what happened at the counselor's office." she said. Um....uh....I.....didn't.....I..... uh.....I......didn't......like.....it.....when.....he...... um......when....he.....uh...touched....me." I barely audibly blubbered through the cries, sniffles, and sobs.

Mrs. Williams had a look of shock and disbelief written all over her face as she sat there watching me cry. She never asked me for any more details and she didn't ask any more questions instead she took me in her arms and cradled me as I cried on her shoulder. I will never forget how safe I felt in her arms. I felt like no one could hurt me as long as she was around. She became my armor and wouldn't let me out of her sight.

After I had calmed down, she moved my desk to put it by hers. She didn't want me out of arms reach and that's where I stayed for the rest of the year. The rest of the day was like slow motion to me. Everyone around me was happy and laughing and doing their work while I sat there with my head down with tears in my eyes feeling defeated and completely dirty while replaying the events of the day over and over and over. I didn't know how to move on from this. I had finally gotten to a point where I was happy and where I felt normal but now all of those things were gone. I was right back to square one trying to find a way out of this dark hole of misery and trying to figure out a way to tell my parents.

As the hours clicked down to minutes and to seconds I became more and more nervous about going home. I still had no idea how I was going to tell them or if I was going to tell them at all. The moment I got home I took a shower to calm my nerves and to attempt getting that dirty feeling off even though I knew it wouldn't happen. How was I going to tell my parents about this? How would they take the news? Would they believe me or push me aside? I didn't know what to do besides go to my room and wait the fateful moment they walked in the door. Around 5:30 they were both home sitting in the living room watching

TV and I knew that this was my one chance to tell them. My heart began to race and my palms began to sweat with anticipation when I finally decided to go talk to them.

I slowly turned the knob on my door and turned left to head to the living room moving at a snails' pace. A million thoughts were running through my head, but the worst one was that they wouldn't believe me. Once I reached the living room I sat down on the couch without saying a word and stared at the TV. Somewhere I found an ounce of courage when I heard a timid voice come out of me and say, "Something happened at school today that I need to tell you about." My father just turned and looked at me like it was an inconvenience for me to talk and for him to mute the TV while my mother just sat there. "What exactly happened?" my father said while staring at the muted TV instead of me. "I was called into the counselors' office." I replied. My mother asked why I was called into his office. "I don't know." I said in a quiet voice. "You were called down there for a reason. Now tell us why. Tell us what you did wrong and how you plan on fixing it." my mother said austerely. "I didn't do anything wrong. He didn't even want to talk to me." I replied assertively. "You must have done something wrong so what did you do?!" she roared. "Mom I didn't do anything wrong. I tried to stop it, but I couldn't." I said. "What exactly did you try to stop?" my father asked. "Um…well I uh tried…..I um tried to get him to stop. I tried to stop him." I said tentatively. "Would you just spit it out already so I can go back to watching TV." said my father. "I'm trying to. I uh didn't....I didn't like it when he...when he touched me there." I said as tears rolled down my cheeks. My father finally turned to look at me, but when he opened his mouth I knew I had done something wrong. "That counselor did not touch you! Don't you say things like that!!!" he shouted. "But dad it's the truth! He pulled my pants down and then he.....he did things to me that I couldn't stop. I couldn't stop it dad. I couldn't." I screamed as the tears were streaming down my face. "Why are you making up a story like this?! How many times have we told you not to make up stories?! Do you just need attention? Because we can give you plenty of attention, but I promise you that you won't like it!!" screamed my mother. "I'm not making up a story! I'm telling you the truth!!! Why don't you believe me? I'm telling the truth!!!!" I screamed as loud as I could. With that scream my father pulled me over his knee and spanked me while shouting at me "You are to tell the truth and not make up stories!! You do not make up stories. You will apologize for lying and you will not do this again!!!!" "Get to your room and think about what really happened at the counselors' office today!" he said when he had finished spanking me. "I don't want to hear another word about this story of yours!" my mother said firmly.

This day had just gone from bad to worse and I couldn't believe it could have gotten any worse. How is it that my teacher believed me, but my parents wouldn't? I was filled with anger, pain, and a deep hurt and I didn't know how to handle it. I didn't know what to do or how to make any of it go away. I wished in that moment for my parents to go away and I didn't care what happened to them. I wished for the pain to go away and for my life to change. I wished for my teacher to show up at my house and take me away from all of this. I wished for a different life through the steady stream of tears flowing from my eyes to the floor.

My mood the next day at school was not much better because I had to tell Mrs. Williams that my parents did not believe me. I had to tell her that they weren't going to do anything about it because they didn't believe me. Without their word it became Mrs. Williams against the counselor. He had been working at that same school for so many years that everyone took his side and no action was taken against him. This meant that I had to go the rest of the year with him there wondering when it was going to happen again. I had to pass him in the halls, hear him call my name, hear his voice, see his face, and pass his office every day. I lived the same nightmare and terror day in and day out just with him being there. It was a daily reminder of the trepidation and pain I felt on that day as well as the anguish and anger I felt when my parents didn't believe me on that fateful day.

TIME TO MOVE

IN THE SUMMER between my sixth and seventh grade years we moved to Neosho, Missouri, the hometown of my father. We had visited this quiet little town numerous of times because my grandparents lived there as well as my aunt and uncle with their families. I was very familiar with this town but had no desire to move there. I had every desire in the world to get out of Fulton, but I would have picked anywhere but Neosho. My father moved down there before my mother, brother and I did because we had to finish out the school year and get our house sold. My father was down there for about six months before we were able to get there. At first I was very excited that he was going to be away. I thought I could relax a little and things would be good, but I quickly found out that would not be so.

While my father was gone, my brother began to hit me and push me around. He would throw me down and beat me up. It seemed as if every day he was doing something to me in some sort of fashion, but I didn't dare confront him about it. During this time my brother seemed to become the man of the house. My mother looked up to him more and I looked down on him more. I didn't really talk much during this time and I didn't really look up at anyone. For the most part I kept my mouth shut and my head down. It seemed like the best plan I could come up with. I didn't want to move to Neosho, but I did want to get out of Fulton. All I really wanted was for everything to stop. For everything to get better. To be happy again. I thought that maybe things would get better when my father was back in the house. When we were all a "family" again.

During that summer we made several trips to Neosho to find a house. While I wasn't excited to go on the first of these trips, I also figured anything could have been better than being at home. At least on the way there and back I had the backseat to myself.

We stayed with my grandma when we went which turned out to be the best thing that could have ever happened to me. I don't know why but my brother never did anything to me while we were there. He didn't touch me, he didn't speak to me, and he didn't look at me. He simply didn't do anything to me at all. It became my soul mission to make sure there was something horribly wrong with each house we went to. The only problem was that nobody in my family ever listened to me. I had to come up with a plan so we could keep coming down here so my brother would leave me alone.

I had come up with a plan that I would just wonder throughout the house while they were looking and start making weird noises. I would hit things, I would scratch the walls, metal, and anything that would make a weird noise. I didn't want it to sound like the typical noises associated with houses, but like something was wrong with the house. This took a great deal more effort than I had anticipated. I did anything and everything I could short of expressing my opinion to sway their decision. I knew in the end it was all a futile attempt, but I couldn't do anything else and I had to do something.

We ended up making five trips in all to house hunt. These trips meant the world to me. They gave me something to hope for; something to look forward to. With each pain filled day that ended I was one day closer to three pain free days. These trips became my safe haven and I endured the pain every day just to get to those three days. Those few days were all I was living for, but at least I had found something to live for.

It was a month before we had to move before my parents decided on a house. A part of me died that day. After every trip my brother always beat me harder than at any other time and now we didn't have any more trips. I didn't have anything to live for now. I was right back to where I started, but this time the sun wasn't coming out from behind the darkness. What hope did I have now?

Each passing day seemed to get worse and worse.

During this time my brother decided that all of his chores became mine and if I didn't get everything done I not only got in trouble with him, but also with my mother. It became impossible for me to get everything done on time and because of that I was in constant pain and fear of what the consequences were going to be.

Moving day finally arrived and by some miracle we were all packed and ready to go. I knew better than to think that this move was going to make everything stop. I only hoped for things to not get worse like they did before. Unlike the first move I didn't have any friends to say good-bye to, nobody to hug, and nobody to care that I was leaving. I prayed during our drive that things would just not get worse. I couldn't imagine things getting any worse, but somehow they always seemed to. I wanted to be happy and to have friends in Neosho. I didn't want to fear anything and I didn't want to constantly be in pain.

Once we got to Neosho it was like we were in fast forward. Everything moved too quickly for me to comprehend what was going on. We got settled into our house and then school started. My brother quickly got involved in activities at school and so did I. I was told to either get involved or walk the 20 miles home every day so I sought out any activity I could. My happiness started to come back when I discovered volleyball. I loved it more than anything and couldn't wait for school to end so I could play. Playing volleyball brought a smile to a face that was so used to frowning. It brought hope when I was hopeless and release when I had no other. Volleyball is what I started to live for. I became absorbed in it, but I never once let my family know how much I liked it. I was afraid they would take it away just like they took away everything else that brought me joy. My life seemed to be climbing its way out of the depths of the valley. The sun began to shine and I started to have friends again. I began to feel normal and like all the other kids. I was amazed by how much things had changed in just a month, but I always had this nagging thought that it was too good to be true. That something was going to happen eventually. After all something always did.

THE FATEFUL NIGHT

IT WAS A Saturday night in September when everything really went wrong. My mother and father told me to clean the bathroom. As any child, I was upset and expressed it in a huff and loud sigh, but knew arguing wouldn't change anything, so I made my way to the bathroom to get started. As I was clearing everything off of the counter, my father came in and pushed me against the wall. I was taken so off guard that I dropped everything in my hands. He quickly grabbed a hold of me and pushed me into the wall again. I didn't know what to think or what was happening. I didn't have any time to think because as soon as I looked up my mother had walked in and joined my father in pushing me. As they kept pushing me I told them to stop and that they were hurting me, but it was useless. It only seemed to upset them more as my father grabbed my hair and threw me out into the hallway. Once I was out there, they both picked me up and took turns slamming my head against the wall. I don't know how many times they did it, but they did it enough to where I was blacking out. I didn't understand what was happening and why they would do this to me. "Please," I cried, "please stop! You're hurting me. Why are you doing this? What did I do? Dad, please stop hurting me!" I said through the tears streaming down my cheeks. My mother evidently didn't think he was doing enough damage as she grabbed me and scratched me with her long, jagged nails until I was bleeding. "Mom, mom why are you doing this? What did I do to make you so angry? Mom, I'm bleeding…..I'm bleeding mom….please stop!" But once again my cries were of no use. It was like they were on a mission of destruction and were not going to stop by my cries. I thought this was going to be the end of it, but instead my father grabbed handfuls of my hair in both hands and dragged me down the hallway as I was kicking, screaming, and grabbing his hands. It was as if he didn't hear my screams and only wanted to inflict more pain when he drug my back over a nail that was up in the hardwood as my mother pushed me down to make sure the nail dug in enough to make me bleed. As I was trying to wrap my mind around this, I realized I was being picked up by my father. *What is he doing? Why is he lifting me up? What is happening? Is he going to throw me? He wouldn't do that….would he. No…no… no….no…*I ended up on the other side of the living room huffing for air. While I was trying to catch my breath, my father walked over to where I was. He bent down, picked me up again and this time I hit the corner of the coffee table. A sharp, intense pain shot from my back and down my legs. This time he stood where he was just watching me trying to breath. I pleaded and begged from them to stop through a waterfall of tears streaming down my face, but I don't know if they even heard me. My mother charged towards me, grabbed a handful of hair and pulled me up until I was looking at her. It was then that she began to slap me continuously for what seemed like forever. My father then came over and punched me in my stomach. I immediately fell to my knees and he took the opportunity to kick me. The only thing I could do was curl up in a ball on the floor and cover my face from the continuous blows. I was coughing profusely and desperately trying to catch my breath. I couldn't see what they were doing, but I felt every bit of it. Then my arms were pulled away from my face as slap after slap landed and then blow after blow to my head was delivered. After a few more kicks to my stomach, they told me to go to my room. I couldn't see straight and I could barely move. It took everything I had to be able to pick myself up and get on two feet without falling over.

Once I was in my room, I was crying uncontrollably. I couldn't believe this had just happened. *What just happened? What was that? What did I do? Those couldn't have been my parents in there. Why didn't they stop when I pleaded them to? Why did they act like they didn't hear my cries? How did I make them so mad? I only huffed about the bathroom but went to go clean it. I didn't say anything else did I? What just happened?? There is so much blood everywhere! This has to be just a bad dream….I'll wake up tomorrow and my body won't hurt.* I won't have bloody arms or back. *I won't have a puffy face and tears making puddles. They didn't even say anything. They didn't say a single word except to go to my room.* All the tissues in my room didn't come close to wiping up all the blood. I knew I needed to get cleaned up, but if I leave my room they could start again. I didn't know what to do. Everything hurt so badly, but the worse physical pain was my head after taking so many blows. I thought I was going to throw up from the amount of constant pain I was in. *How am I going to wash all of this off? How am I going to go to church tomorrow?*

That night after I knew they were sound asleep I went to the bathroom to find all the medicine I needed and got a few wet washcloths. As quickly and quietly as I possibly could I went back to my room. *Oh no, somebody is up! Where do I put all of this?* I stuffed everything into my pillowcase and acted like I was asleep. As I heard the footsteps get closer and closer, my heart began to beat faster and harder. Just then the footsteps stopped and my door opened. My father walked over to my bed as my heart beat so fast and hard that I thought for sure he could hear it. I only wanted him to go away and was wondering what he was doing in here anyway, but I quickly found out as he punched me as hard as he could in my stomach. Immediately my eyes popped open and all I could see was my father looking down at me. He punched me a few more times and then turned and walked out. *What was that about? Haven't you already done enough damage without adding that? He didn't even say anything again. Suzanne, focus and try to breathe. Slow, steady breaths. Slow. Slow. One breath at a time. What did I do? I did what they told me to do. I did have a little of an attitude but I still tried to do what they told me to. There's no way that I can go to church in just a few short hours. I'm so confused and tired.*

THE NEXT DAY

FINALLY MORNING CAME and it was a new day. This won't happen again, I thought. It was all just a crazy dream, but I knew deep down that wasn't true. Now I had to figure out how I was going to stand up straight and cover everything up. I didn't come out of my room until five minutes before we had to leave for church...just enough time to brush my teeth. *Maybe nothing will happen.* They acted like last night never happened, like it was a dream...but I had the scrapes, headaches, and bruises to prove it. Now I had to get in the car with them, go to church, and act like everything is just fine? *Yeah right! There's no way I can do that! How am I going to do this? What if they do something to me on the way there? There's no way I can pull it together in time for church if they do. Why are they acting like everything is fine? Should I act like that too? I can't do that!* "Suzanne,

41

it's time to leave" said my father. "We're going to be late if you don't hurry up" said my mother. Within seconds I was out in the car ready for church while still trying to figure everything out. The normal five-minute drive seemed to last forever. *Is he driving slower than normal or am I just paranoid?* Finally we got there, but I still wasn't ready to face everybody. One thing was for certain, I wasn't going to sit with them for anything. Now all I had to do was to put that into practice, but I had class time to figure that out and to find some courage. After class I stayed and talked to my friends longer than usual. My goal was to walk into worship late so that it would be easier for me to sit on the back pew. As everything developed, I was quite surprised when my plan actually worked and I took a seat next to my friend, Charlotte.

I knew church wasn't going to be easy because not only is my father a deacon, but he is also the song leader. I would have to watch him up on that stage after he beat me the night before. Normally I love to sing and would have sung, but this Sunday there were too many thoughts running through my head. *He is such a hypocrite! How can he go up there like nothing ever happened? Does he know how much he and mom hurt me? Don't cry Suzanne…just don't cry and call more attention to yourself.* All I could do was sit in the pew and think about last night. No matter how hard I tried to fight the tears, they soon began rolling down my cheeks. Charlotte finally got me out of the pew and into the bathroom. "Suzanne, what's wrong?" she asked in a very concerned voice, but all I could do was cry.

"You aren't going to believe me anyway." I said through the sobs. "Please just tell me, Emma." Jess said. "I will believe you, I promise." *Should I really tell her? What if they find out? What will they do? Maybe it was only a one time thing… then maybe not. She's obviously worried. I should just tell her.* After calming down enough to talk I reluctantly told her what had happened. She stared at me with her mouth wide open and her eyes as big as they could possibly be. "What?!" she exclaimed. " Are you serious?!" "I told you that you wouldn't believe me" through the tears forming in my eyes and disappointment in my tone. "I just don't understand. Why would they do this to you?" I wanted to tell her that it was all just a nightmare. That it didn't really happen, but my body was pulling me back to reality with every ache and pain. I knew I had to show her some proof so she would believe the words I was saying. Very slowly as tears streamed like a river down my face into a puddle I rolled up my sleeves to reveal the scratches my mother had administered. It looked like I was in the middle of two cats fighting. My arms were bright red with open gashes from my biceps to my wrists. Charlotte delicately took my arms in her hands and inspected them, looking up and down and turning them over and over again in her hands. In a whisper she asked if my mother had done this to me. I leaned back against the wall contemplating if I should tell her. I looked at her and to my arms and back to her and back to my arms. She had this look of disbelief and pain as she kept looking at my arms. I finally said yes in a far quieter whisper than hers. With that answer she took me and wrapped her arms around me embracing me with a hug. It was then when I realized how tired and weak, and how much pain I was in. We both slumped to the ground as I cried on her shoulder. All I wanted to know was what I had done wrong and if this was going to happen again. "What did I do wrong, Charlotte?" I asked through the sobs. "I don't know." was her only answer.

I sat there trying to control my tears as Charlotte consoled me silently while she kept looking at my arms as she tried to take it all in. I was so preoccupied with my thoughts bouncing from one thing to the next and over to something else that I didn't even notice that someone had walked into the bathroom. I knew that some way I was going to have to quit crying and find a way to look halfway presentable, but before I could deal with that I had to get Charlotte's word. "Please don't tell anyone about this! I don't know what will happen if anyone knows about it. Please, please don't tell anyone." I begged and pleaded of her. She obliged by promising to not tell anyone. With that she helped me get up, wipe my eyes and cheeks of all the tears, and try to not look like Rudolph. "You don't even look like you've been crying." she said, but we both knew she was lying.

As soon as we got out of the bathroom we quickly joined our circle of friends hoping that no one would notice we were gone. This ray of hope was quickly shattered when I saw my father spot me and come over to me with a look in his eye that screamed I was in trouble. As soon as we got into the car the yelling and interrogation started. They were both yelling and asking questions at the same time while expecting answers. I didn't know if I should answer or just sit there and listen. "Why didn't you sit with us? Where were you when church started? Where were you when church ended? Where were you during church? Why does your face look like that? What have you been doing? We go to church for a reason and you are to be in church! Why do we go to church? Answer me when I ask you a question. You are not to be somewhere else in the building during worship! What were you thinking? Don't you dare interrupt me again little miss priss! Why did you and Charlotte leave? What were you two doing that was so important? What did you talk to her about? When we go to church you are to be on time and sit where we tell you to sit. You don't get to sit wherever your little heart desires to sit. We are the parents, not you. You don't get to make those decisions." When I sat there and listened, I was yelled at and then when I tried to answer them I was yelled at for interrupting them. *They should know why I didn't sit with them. They should know what they did last night. They have to know what they did last night. There's no way that they don't know what they did....so why are they acting like this?* Answer us! *I know we're in church for a reason, but they haven't really been acting like Christians lately. He went up there and led singing after beating me last night like nothing was wrong. Like he did nothing wrong. And now they're yelling at me for trying to figure all of this out. What are they thinking? That's the question I should be asking them. I should be asking them what's wrong with them. It shouldn't be the other way around.* ANSWER US NOW!!!

THE NEXT DAY   45

"I went to the bathroom with Charlotte because I started crying during church. I was talking with my friends for longer than expected so I didn't get into worship in time, so I just sat in the back with Jess and her family. I didn't want to walk to the front and make a big deal out of it, so I just sat with her." I said as I was trying unsuccessfully to not have a tone. *Are they kidding me?! Suzanne, you have to calm down. Having a tone isn't going to help matters and you're already in enough trouble as it is. Apologize and do it quickly before things get any worse.* "I'm sorry for having a tone." I said in the most sincere voice I could muster up. "It's too late for that now! said my mother. *Great. Just great. Now what's going to happen when we get home and behind closed doors? I wish this ride would last longer just so I don't have to be home with them. That's the last place I want to be right now. Do they know that I told Charlotte? And here's the house…what's going to happen now that they are mad?* "Get in the house now!" shouted my father while he was putting the car in park. *Here it comes.*

I went to my room and put on some old clothes as fast as I possibly could so my church clothes wouldn't be ruined. The second I put my shirt on, my father came barging in my room and slapped me as hard as he could across my face. At least that's what it felt like to me as the tears immediately welled up in my eyes. As I moved my hand up to my face he punched me in my stomach. *Can't I just get a break here?!?!* The only thing I could do was double over in pain, but that wasn't something he was going to allow happening. Instead he straightened me up by

EXTRACTING SUZANNE

grabbing a handful of hair and while keeping me straight with that handful he punched me over and over and over again. *Please just stop. Please. If I throw up on him who knows what will happen. Stop! What did I do so wrong?* Just when I thought I was going to throw up on him he finally stopped. *Thank you God.* He finally let go of my hair and I fell down to the ground holding my stomach.

I laid there on the hard floor in the fetal position as tears were coming down my cheeks. *What is happening?* I didn't lay there long before my father was back and grabbing my legs, but this time instead of dragging me he lifted me off of the ground and then dropped me. I put my arms out to break my fall, but that only caused my wrists to be bent back. I quickly decided I couldn't do that again, but how was I going to break my fall? He picked me up again and this time I put my forearms out so I wouldn't hit my head. I was successful in breaking my fall, but I was also successful in sending shivers down my arms. He grabbed my legs again and this time started to drag me out of my room and towards the living room which only meant one thing…. that nail. *Not this nail again! Please! It's like a knife stabbing me and then moved along my back. It feels like my back is being ripped open. Please go the other way around. Please go the other way….the other way!!! Please….NOOOOOO…. AHHHHHHHHHHH NOOOOOOO!!!!! Please make it stop!!! Make it stop!!!!! Make it stop!!! AHHHHHH!!!!!! STOP IT!!! It's too much!!!*

This pain is too much! I can't do this. Why are they doing this? I can't breathe. There's so much blood. God please don't let them do that again. I can't go through that again. Oh please God. Please. My mother towered over me as I was writhing in pain and gasping for breath through the tears and screams. She stood there watching me squirm and listen to my screams without the slightest bit of sympathy or guilt. She must have decided that I was not in enough pain because she started to kick me full force. "YOU.... ARE....A...FILTHY....BITCH! WE...GIVE...YOU... EVERTHING....BUT...YOU...DON'T...DO...A... DAMN........THING....FOR...US!" she shouted out with each kick. I tried but to no avail block the kicks as best I could. The only thing I was successful in was blocking them from my face. Suddenly she stopped. *Is it over? Can I leave now? Can I go throw up now?* "STAND UP!" my father shouted. *Stand up?! Who is he kidding? Stand up after all of that? I can't stand up!* "STAND UP!!! I won't tell you again!!!" he shouted as he inched closer and closer to me. I was already rolled over on my side so I thought I could just put my knee out and try to push myself up, but my body was not having it. Between the blows to my stomach, the tear in my back, my wrists, the blurry vision, and the soreness from last night I was struggling, but knew I had to find some way to get up. I was trying my best to push through the pain but was moving pretty slow and evidently too slow for my fathers' liking. He yanked me up and pushed me against the wall. I tried to grab his hands, but my mother held them down. I tried to kick, but he put his legs against mine. I was pinned against the wall. He stared into my panicked eyes with his cold eyes and then squeezed my neck with his hand. He began to squeeze tighter and tighter. *No! What! This isn't happening! This is a dream! I can't breathe! I can't swallow! Stop it! Quit! I can't move! The more I try the tighter he squeezes! I can't breathe! I can't swallow! I can't breathe! I can't breathe! I can't breathe! Is he going to kill me? He is going to kill me. He's going to watch me die. Can't breathe!! Open your eyes! OPEN YOUR EYES!!! Please God, let him let go of me. Make him stop. Stop! Please.....*

I don't know when I passed out, how long I was out, or when he let up, but when I came to I saw them towering over me. I instantly grabbed my neck and could feel the heat from his hand still there. I tried to take a deep breath, but that hurt too much. I was afraid that he might do that again and I wanted to breathe while I had the chance. "You don't deserve to live! But you aren't worth me going to jail over either! You aren't worth anything!! You're just a worthless piece of shit that nobody cares about!" they shouted. "Go to your room right now!" screamed my father. With that I slowly peeled myself off of the ground and walked toward my room. Once I was in there I felt a second of relief followed by shear pain. *Do they know that I told Charlotte about last night? I can barely walk. I wish I had a bed to lie on. Something better than this hardwood floor. I can't believe how much pain I am in. I'm glad I stashed some medicine from last night. What have I done to cause this? I'm a worthless piece of shit....did they really just say that to me? Maybe I should just sleep and then everything will get better. He chocked me...he really chocked me. What if he does that again?*

THE NEXT DAY   49

TAKE A CHANCE

LATER THAT DAY, I made the risky decision to go out of my room to go to the bathroom and to apologize for whatever I had done to make them so mad. I slowly crept my way on my tiptoes to the living room to see what they were doing and what kind of mood they might be in. They were both sitting in their chairs watching TV and didn't look like they were mad anymore. *Try to sound as sincere as possible....just be sincere. Maybe if they believe me I will be able to figure out how I made them so mad. If they ask what I'm sorry for just say for what happened at church....that should cover it. Ok here we go....be sincere.* "Mom and dad" I said in a timid voice, "I'm sorry for making you so upset." *Just go ahead and tell them what you're sorry for. Better to be proactive about this....I think.* "I shouldn't have come into church late and I shouldn't have gone to the bathroom with Charlotte throughout service. I'm sorry." I said in what I thought was a convincing voice. "You're damn right you're sorry." said my father without batting an eye. "You embarrassed us by not being in church and you made your mother sit by herself." he continued. "I know and I'm sorry for that." I said in the same convincing voice. *Please just let everything be okay now.* "Did we tell you to come out of your room? said my mother stonily. "No, you didn't. I just wanted to apologize and it's time for church." I said. "We aren't going to church just for you to embarrass us more." said my father in a low, demanding voice. "I want to go to church. That's what we are supposed to do." I said. "Well you didn't think that you had to go to church this morning apparently." said my mother sarcastically. "I could still hear everything that was going on, but something came up and we had to go handle it." I said. I was trying my best to not tell them that I told Charlotte about what had happened. I was becoming more and more annoyed by this whole situation and was having a hard time controlling the tone of my voice. "You will not embarrass us anymore so we are not going to church tonight." said my father in that same low and demanding voice. "I am going to go to church tonight. It is what we are supposed to do and it would feel wrong if I did not go." I said in grave voice. What I really wanted to tell them is that I am afraid to stay here alone with you and would love an hour of peace. An hour of peace is why I want to go to church. I don't want to go to church for any other reason except for a moment of peace. "What did you just say?" said my father as he snapped around and stared at me. *Well I'm in too deep now so I might as well just keep going.* "I said I am going to church. "No you aren't!" he shouted back. "You don't have to take me or pick me up. I'll just call Kevin (our youth minister) to come and pick me up." I said. "No! No, you will NOT do that!!" he yelled. "Dad, it's really not a big deal for him to come get me. You don't have to get out and isn't this the reason why we were fighting earlier.... me not being in church? And now I'm trying to go and you're trying to stop me? That doesn't make sense." I said verging on screaming. "You will NOT go to church!! Do I make myself clear?!" "No it doesn't make sense at all." I said in a sharp tone. *Great job Suzanne. Have a tone with him because that will really make things better. I just want to go to church to get away from them. With the way they are acting you would think they would jump at the chance for me to be away.* "I'm just trying to go to church like you have told me to and I'm trying to make it as easy for you as possible." I said in a much calmer tone.

I don't know what happened or why it happened. I knew I was defeated in this fight. I didn't have a dog in it, but I fought it like I did. I'm not really sure why I chose to fight it so hard besides I just wanted to get away from them. I didn't want to be anywhere near them anymore; at least for an hour. I just wanted to get away from it all and went to great lengths to accomplish that. I never thought they would have let me go to church, but for some strange reason they let me and I never questioned them about it. I was so happy and confused by their decision, but I now had a little time to not worry or think about it at all. Not seeing my parents at church put me at ease and mollified my emotions. I finally had a peaceful second to myself and I soaked it in as much as I possibly could.

I didn't have to ride in the car with them or sit with them. I didn't have to see my father leading singing. I didn't have to calculate every move or every word. I felt free being away from their ever watchful eyes. For the first time I felt like I could breathe, like I could relax my shoulders and not worry about what was going to happen.

As my peaceful second drew closer to an end I couldn't help but think about what kind of mood my parents would be in once I got home. I kept trying to answer why they let me go tonight. I didn't want my peace to end but knew that it had to. I kept wondering what would happen when I got home. If maybe they had bottled it all up and were waiting to explode until I got there. *Maybe nothing will happen. Nothing happened when I asked about going to church. Yeah, there was a lot of yelling and fighting, but nothing physical. What does that mean? What's going on with them? What did I do?*

All too soon my peaceful hour and a half grew to a close when Kevin pulled up to my house. I thought that if I just walked in the house, said hey, went about my business and left them alone things would be fine. "Hey mom and dad." I said in an upbeat voice. "I'm pretty tired and have some homework to do so I'm going to go take a shower, finish my homework, and go to bed." Before I could even turn to walk down the hall my mother asked me how church was. "It was good." I replied. "Nothing exciting happened, but some people asked where you were." I knew immediately that I should not have said that last statement because my father spun around in his chair and demanded for me to tell them what I told everyone. "I just told them that you weren't feeling well." I said still trying to figure out why he spun around in his chair so fast. "So you lied to them?" asked my mother in a sharp tone. And with that statement I knew I was in trouble. There was no way for me to get out of this and I now understood why he spun around so quickly. "Yeah. I guess I did. What was I supposed to say?" I asked in a confused voice. *Great job Suzanne! Way to open your mouth! Maybe I shouldn't have even said hi to them.* "You tell them the truth!" barked my father. "So I was supposed to tell them that you didn't want to go to church and you finally let me go?" I asked in that same confused voice. "Don't be a smartass!" shouted my mother. *I've got to figure out a way out of this before they rip me into pieces. How do I back out of this? Think quicker Suzanne. You've got to be faster if you want to get out of here alive.* "Okay, you're right. I'm sorry." I said. "I'm just going to go take a shower real quick, finish my homework, and go to bed. I'm sorry for upsetting you." "Are you the adult? Are you the parent?" asked my father sarcastically. I didn't know whether to answer his questions or to just wait. I decided to wait as he stared at me and finally shouted "I asked you a question! You answer me!" "No, I'm not." I replied in a disheartening tone partly because I knew I wasn't going to be leaving here any time soon and because

I felt so completely helpless.

"That's right! You don't tell us what you're going to do! You ask us if you can do something little miss priss!" shouted my father. "Can I go take a shower and go to bed?" I asked. "No you may not!" he said. I didn't know what to do. I didn't even know how we got to this point. What turn of events caused us to get here? I just stood there dumbfounded looking at my father and my mother not knowing what else to do. "You get over here right now!" he barked. *Great now what? I thought this was over for tonight. What is he going to do now?* "GET OVER HERE!" he shouted since I evidently wasn't walking fast enough. As soon as I got to where he was sitting, he grabbed my arm and threw me over his legs. *He's not really going to… going to spank me is he? All for wanting to take a shower and go to bed. What is he doing? He's not taking off his belt is he? No way is he really going to do this. How many times is he going to hit me? There's no way to wiggle out of his grip. I can't believe he's going to do this….and he just did. This is humiliating and painful. Just get through it without crying. Be tough.* There was no way for me to contain my cries and screams while he struck me full force. I had lost count around 20 and it felt like it lasted an eternity after that. When he finally stopped my face was beat red and stained with tears. He made me stand there in front of him until he told me I could go take a shower. I would have much rather taken punches over that. That was a whole different level of pain. It was humiliating and degrading and made me feel worthless.

Finally! Just get in and out as quickly as possible. Did he really just do that? I mean really did he just do that? That was awful. This whole weekend has been horrible. I was just to a point where I was starting to be happy again and then this happens. Why can't I just be happy? Why do they have to constantly knock me farther and farther down? Just hurry up and get to bed. Maybe the quicker I do things, the better they will be. It may help if they see less of me. I don't know what to do. I feel like years have passed from Friday to today! I'm so glad I have school tomorrow! Within shear minutes I was in my room trying to figure out how I was going to sit and do my homework. Sitting was out of the question tonight so I laid down on my stomach to finish my homework by the glow of a flashlight. I didn't want my light to be on because they would be more likely to walk in and I couldn't handle anything else tonight. I couldn't focus on any of my work and finally put it up after re-reading the same question five times. *Everything has changed. Everything. Nothing has been great, but now this? My father tried to punch me in the face when I was little and I remember him pulling his hand out of the wall, but now this. Does he really hate me this much? What did I do to him? Was I wrong to cover for them tonight? If I had told everyone the truth I probably would have gotten it worse. Why do they hate me? Why?*

Just when I thought everything was going to be fine and they were going to leave me alone for the rest of the night, the man that was supposed to love me and protect me came barging into my room. *Please go away. Please go away. Please go away.* As much as I wished him away he only crept closer and closer. He grabbed me by my hair and yanked me up. He then punched me and threw me to the ground then grabbed me by my hair again, but this time started to drag me once again. "What are you doing?!" I screamed, but it had no effect on him. *I can't go over that nail again. Not tonight for sure. Why can't he just stop? Why doesn't he listen to me or even act like he hears me? We're heading straight for that nail.* I grabbed onto everything possible to keep from going over that nail again. I sprawled my legs and hooked my feet into doorways and tried to stop being drug with my hands. Everything I tried only made him more mad, but I was desperate. I had to try something. I couldn't do this again. *Please just stop and let me go back to bed. I wasn't even doing anything wrong!* We got to where that nail was and I tried my best to brace for the indescribable pain. "Dad, please don't do this. Just stop please!" I screeched. "Dad! Please stop! Dad! Stop this!!" My outcries only made him push down harder and pull me over that nail more. I never knew I could hate an inanimate object so much, but I had such a deep hatred for that nail. *Oh please make this stop! Why won't he stop? Why does he like hurting me? Please stop! Please make this come to an end. I can't handle this!* With each push and pull I lost my breath from the shear pain he was causing and gasped for air. I writhed in pain and tried to wiggle free from his firm grasp. *Hasn't he already done enough tonight? God, make him hear my cries. Make him see my face. Make him see the pain he's causing me. When will he stop? When my shirt is completely ripped off?* I didn't know that I could cry as much and as hard as I had in the past 24 hours. I was completely exhausted and every part of me ached.

Before I even had time to thank God for making him stop, this man picked me up and threw me down on my back. As I landed desperately trying to breathe a whole new sense of pain surged through me. Once I landed he picked me up again and threw me down time after time after time while I was frantically trying to catch my breath before he threw me again. The last time he picked me up he threw me into the corner of the table as a piercing pain started from my back and spread out to my fingertips and toes. He loomed over me as I laid on the ground with blood pooling under me trying to breathe. He bent down and peeled me off of the ground then pushed me against the wall. This man began to punch me over and over again until he let go of me and I collapsed onto the ground defeated. Once I was down on the ground he thrust his foot into my side time and time again. Tears were rolling down my cheeks as I tried my best to block his blows any way that I could. "Shut up you little bitch! Quit that ridiculous crying! I'm not hurting you in any way! I said to shut up damn it! Listen to me! I am your father! Shut up or I will give you something to cry about! You're nothing but a worthless piece of shit and a huge mistake! I said to shut the fuck up!" He bellowed. *Quit crying. Just quit crying. What does he mean he isn't hurting me? He's kicking the crap out of me, but he's not hurting me??? How crazy is he?? He's not supposed to be doing this! Please just stop doing this and let me go to bed. This isn't a father. This isn't a dad. This is a monster that is in your nightmares.* He picked me up by my hair and spit in my face whilst telling me to get to bed. "Don't you make a sound in there! I don't want to hear you at all!"

I quickly walked to my room and quietly shut my door. I couldn't believe the condition my shirt was in and was afraid to see at what my back was going to look like. I finally looked in the mirror and saw jagged gashes that were coursing out blood all up and down my back. It was a deep crimson color with more cuts than I could count. I just stared in that mirror speechless with my mouth gaping open. I had never seen anything like that and didn't know it could have happened to me. *How do I clean this? What do I even do or where do I begin?* Once I finally stopped bleeding I put Neosporin on as many cuts as I could and then went to bed. *Maybe he won't come in here this time. Maybe he'll go to sleep and not bother me for the rest of the night and hopefully I can get some sleep. Oh I'm so tired. Why doesn't he do this to my brother? If he did I at least wouldn't feel so worthless and question everything so much. Why can't I be more like my brother? Everything would be fine if I were. Why can't he love me too? Why didn't she do anything besides sit there and watch her husband beat up her daughter? She just sat there and cheered him on. They don't deserve the title of mom or dad. That implies someone who actually loves their child.*

God, please just let me get some sleep tonight and quit thinking about all of this. Why did you put me in this family? Why am I such a mistake? Why don't the people that are supposed to love me, love me? What did I do so wrong? Please don't allow for me to get beat tomorrow. Help me to choose my words wisely and to be soft spoken so I don't offend anyone. Please help them to have a good day at work and for them to not be stressed when they come home. Please make my brother stay away from me and not cause anything. Please don't let him lie to them to intentionally get me into trouble. Please just help tomorrow to go well and for none of this to happen again. Please help me get some sleep tonight. Please. In Jesus name amen.

I laid awake until I heard them go to bed and waited until I knew they were asleep before I let myself relax enough to close my eyes. As soon as my eyes closed I drifted off to sleep but before I knew it morning had come. When my alarm sounded those oh so annoying beeps it took every fiber of my being to turn it off. Once it was off I laid there not believing it was already morning and wondered what they were going to be like today. While trying to get ready and be as quiet as possible so I wouldn't wake anybody my body screamed at me to quit moving. The aches and the pains were just too much to bear. I had never been in this amount of pain or this sore before. I tried to stand up straight, but I just couldn't bear the pain. I wondered how I was going to get through the school day and volleyball practice after. Somehow as the morning went on I pushed the pain aside and slowly finished getting ready for the day.

I went straight back to my room to wait until it was time to leave. *Maybe I should just leave now and walk to school. I wouldn't have to see them and they wouldn't have to see me. They wouldn't have to drop me off and that would be much easier for them. But then again what if that made them mad? What would it be like when I got back home? Or maybe this weekend was kind of a one-time kind of deal, but then again probably not. That's just wishful thinking.* While I was still debating leaving I heard my father get up. I prayed with all of my heart that he wouldn't come into my room. Then I heard him stop in front of my door and I froze. He turned the doorknob and my heart sank. I didn't dare look up at him. I only thought that maybe if I didn't make eye contact then maybe nothing would happen. And for the first time since all of this started I was right. He was nice. He was gentle. He was cordial. It was uncanny and creepy. That was not at all what I was expecting and now it had me wondering why he was so nice. I sat in my room trying to figure all of this out until it was time to go. I thought that maybe this whole weekend was a dream, but my body told me otherwise. I thought maybe he wouldn't do any of that again, but my mind told me otherwise. I thought maybe he loved me and cared about me again, but my heart told me otherwise.

As soon as I shut my car door he asked, "Why were you already up and ready for school?" I said, "I just woke up and couldn't go back to sleep so I decided to just get ready." He seemed pleased by this answer and didn't ask me anymore questions. I was very thankful for this. I was even more thankful when we pulled up to the school because this meant ten hours away from them. Right before

I opened my door he said to me in a chilling voice, "Stay quiet and don't even think about telling anyone about what goes on in our house. That's for us to know and for no one to find out. Is that clear?" "Yes." I said in a crushed voice. As I walked into school I couldn't help but to think things were going to be bad once I got back home.

THE LONG DAY

WHILE WALKING INTO school I didn't know what to think. I was for sure that everyone around me would be able to tell that something was wrong either by my attempts at hiding the pain or by my bloodshot eyes. When anyone came near I became paranoid and immediately put my head down hoping they wouldn't talk to me. My father's voice kept ringing loud and clear in my head. I didn't want to do anything that could possibly get back to him or make him upset. The hardest part about that day was trying to stay awake during my classes. Every part of me wanted to go to sleep and forget about what was happening; to dream the day away.

With each passing minute I couldn't help but think that was one minute closer to going home. I kept wondering what it was going to be like when I got home. What they were going to be like and what would happen.

When my father picked me up I quickly learned what kind of mood he was in and it was far from good. I don't know what happened, but I knew not to talk unless spoken to. I sat silently in the car on the way home not looking at him. I was trying my best to stay quiet and not seen. When we rolled onto our driveway and the car came to a stop my father yelled at me to get inside. I quickly went in and went to my room thinking that's what he wanted me to do, but evidently that was the wrong decision as he pulled me by my hair into the kitchen. "Look at all of these dishes! Why have you not done these yet? Why is this kitchen such a mess? Why have you not cleaned it up yet? When you got up this morning you should have cleaned up this kitchen instead of sitting in your room! Why don't you think? Why are you so selfish? Do you think that the world revolves around you? You are so incredibly selfish! Get this cleaned up right now!" he roared. I stood there looking at him dumbfounded not knowing what to think, but I knew exactly what I needed to do. I began to walk to the sink to start washing the dishes, but he grabbed my arm and stopped me in my tracks. *What is he doing? I am trying to do what he just told me to do. I didn't even argue with him. It wouldn't have made a difference anyway.* He pulled me closer to him and then with one sharp gesture he threw me into the cabinets. My lower back hit the top of the counter as the back of my head hit the cabinets. He then came over to me, grabbed my arm, and with another swift gesture threw me into the cabinets again. Before I could even try to control my body from hitting he was grabbing my arm and throwing me once again.

Just as suddenly as he started he stopped. I seized the opportunity to gather myself and calm down as best as I could. I hadn't even noticed that he had opened up a drawer and pulled something out of it. He walked over to me with an eerie smile across his face. *Is that a knife in his hand? That is a knife! What he is doing with that? Why is he smiling? Why is he walking towards me? Why is he coming closer? Stop walking! Stop getting closer! Why is he holding a knife? What is he going to do to me? What is he going to do? Oh God please no! Please stop whatever it is he's going to do! Please make him stop! What is going to happen? What is he doing? Please God make him stop!* My eyes were fixated on the knife he was holding so firmly in his right hand as he continued to get closer. He stopped not even six inches away from me and I was frozen in fear. I couldn't make my body move. My head was screaming at me to find a way out of this. To find a way to put one foot in front of the other and run, but I was petrified with fear. In one swift movement he thrust his left hand up to my neck and pushed my head against the cabinet and with the other he brought the knife up to my face. *What is he going to do? Is he going to kill me? Oh God please make this all go away! Make the knife go away! Make him go away!* He pushed the end of the knife into my left cheek just far enough to break the skin and draw blood. He then stroked the blade from the top of my forehead down my neck while holding me still. Once he pushed the knife into my cheek I became fixated on his eyes hoping that he could see me pleading through my eyes for him to stop. He then brought the knife back up to my cheek and pushed the end in a little more this time. It was like he was mesmerized with the blood and my fear stricken body. I wanted to run. I wanted to yell for him to stop and take that knife away, but I couldn't make my body move. He then slid the blade from the blood down my cheek and this time stopped at my lips and just stared at me. Then ran the blade over my lips and back down my neck where he stopped and pushed the blade into my neck. He moved closer to me and said in a low, raspy, cruel voice "You get this kitchen cleaned up right now or I will come back with this knife and I promise it will hurt a lot more. You'll have more than one spot that is bleeding for sure. You have 30 minutes to have this place spotless or you will have something to cry about. This was your one and only warning. You now have 29 minutes!"

Once he let go of me I realized that I had been holding my breath in fear, but I didn't have time to gather my thoughts or catch my breath. All I knew was that I had to get this kitchen spotless and move at lightning speed to accomplish that. I washed dishes faster than I had ever washed dishes before. I wiped down the counters and the stove with a fierce determination. I ran as fast as I could while blood was still coming down my face to get the broom and mop. I had just finished mopping when my father came back in with the knife still in his hand. I was out of breath and frantic that he would find something wrong just so he could use that knife but was surprised when he turned and left without saying a word. I looked over the kitchen and was relieved that he didn't find anything wrong. It was then when I finally took a breath and silently thanked God for not allowing that knife to be used on my face.

I quickly, but quietly went into my room wanting just a moment to myself. I longed to be back at school and away from him. At least there I wasn't being threatened with knives or thrown against the walls. Slowly I turned to look at my face in the mirror and became absorbed in examining the cut he created. I began to imagine what my face would look like with cuts all over it from that knife and how deep he would cut me. I imagined what the scars would look like and how nobody would ever want to look at me again. I began to imagine the amount of extreme pain I would go through and decided that I had to do everything in my power to keep that knife as far away as I could.

Things didn't turn out any better when my mother walked in the door not long after I had gotten into my room for she too was in a foul mood. Before she even went to the living room she was in my room yelling at me. "What do you think you are doing in here? This house is a mess! Why do you think you should be in here and not cleaning up? You are such a lazy, filthy bitch! Your father and I work all day long and you don't do a damn thing! You just think you can do whatever your little selfish heart pleases! You will get this house cleaned from top to bottom immediately! Why are you still standing there? Didn't

I make myself clear?! Get to cleaning now!" As I was trying to walk past her to get started she also grabbed my arm and pulled me close to her. She just stood there staring at me for what seemed like an eternity and then slapped me across my face. Tears instantly formed and threatened to fall down my cheeks as she slapped me harder. This time those tears did fall down while more were forming and that only made her more mad. I put my hands up to my face to deter some of her blows but she only pushed me into a corner and kept hitting me with more force. She then grabbed a handful of hair in each hand and began to bash my head into the wall while screaming at me to quit crying or she would give me something to cry about.

Then she said it. She called for him to come in and help her shut me up. *No please don't come in. Be too tired to deal with me. Don't come in here. Why is she doing this to me? When did it become my job to clean everything? I was only minding my own business. He isn't too tired. Go away!! Please just go away!! She's already doing enough without you coming to her aide!* "Please just let me go clean and I will leave you both alone." I pleaded. They evidently had a different idea in mind when my father kicked my kneecap and my mother smiled watching me fall to the ground holding my knee. My father then pushed my shoulders down while holding my arms above my head as my mother stood over me. She then lifted her leg and slammed her foot on my rib cage as I shrieked. I tried to squirm out of my fathers' grip, turn or do anything to find a way to cover my stomach to block her blows that were alternating between my ribcage and stomach, but with every attempt his grip only got tighter. *Don't do it again! Please stop!* She then moved up to my chest and brought her foot down with great force over and over and over again all the while my father is telling her to keep going until I quit being such a baby. *Shut up! Shut up! Shut up!! Stop!* "Start kicking her side." he said in an almost excited voice. *No! Don't listen to him! Listen to my cries! Listen to me!* "No please don't! I will go clean right now and it will be spotless!" I said in a breathless plea.

My brother had now come home and heard all of the screeching. He came into my room to see my father holding my arms over my head, my mother looming over me, and me helpless with a red face as tears streamed down onto the floor. "Hold her legs down." my father said to him as he immediately held them down, but not without a struggle as I kicked him and did everything I could do to make it harder for him. As soon as I was pinned down she began to kick my side with as much force as she could. "Please stop! Stop. Please. Please." I begged in between kicks. My ribs were on fire and I couldn't handle much more. It was getting harder to breathe and everything I tried was immediately put to an end. *They have to stop. This is too much.* My father asked my brother if he wanted to get me back for kicking him. He promptly switched positions with my mother and began to kick me in the same place that she was. He then stepped over me and began to kick my other side while my father and my mother held me down. While they watched their son kick me and listened to my never ending cries of pain. None of them were satisfied until I was completely exhausted and couldn't move anymore. That is when my mother and father let go of me and when my brother stopped kicking me. "Get up and clean this house now! It had better be spotless by the time you go to bed!" they said before they turned and left.

I feebly laid there unable to move or even think about moving. I didn't understand what had just happened or why it happened. *I was in my own room not bothering anyone minding my own business and then this happened. What did I do to cause them to do this? What did I do? How am I going to get off of this floor or clean this house? I can't move... not right now. I can't even roll over on my side much less get up and clean, but what if I don't get up? How much worse will it get? Will he get that knife again? What will they do? What will they do to me? Oh God please help me get up. Help me push the pain aside. Help me to get this house clean and to find a way to ease the pain. Help me to find a way to breathe without this piercing pain. God please help me get up off of this floor.*

I winced just thinking about getting off of the floor but was too afraid not to. I decided that I had to somehow get up or they would come in here and who knows what would happen then. I painstakingly rolled onto my right side and placed my left hand around my side hoping to give a little cushion. I slowly pulled my knees up to my chest wincing with every movement. I had now put myself in the fetal position and had exerted all of my energy and wasn't even standing yet. A million thoughts were running through my head while trying to catch my breath and find some sort of energy. My only goal at the moment was trying to get up. I was going to count that as a victory at the moment, but I had their voices ringing in the back of my head and my body screaming that it can't take anymore tonight. After a few more minutes I finally chose to attempt getting up. I rolled my left knee down to the ground and pushed myself up with both my knee and my left hand. I had now gotten to all fours and was once again out of breath forcing me to take another break. Once I got a little air I was determined to stand this time. Little by little I made progress and was standing on two feet but wasn't able to stand straight. I was in pure agony just standing there leaned against the wall. I could barely breathe or move at all.

I had to come up with a plan on how I was going to get this house cleaned. On how I was going to move and breathe all at the same time. I thought if I could just get my mind on anything besides what has been going on I could push the pain far enough back so I could function. I was going to have to move quickly and precisely in order for the house to pass their inspection. With each step I took toward my door I became more and more determined to succeed. I was going to get this done and fear was purely my motivation.

I reluctantly turned the doorknob knowing there was no turning back now. In my head I made a list of everything that needed to be done and how much time each item would most likely take if there were no problems. Starting laundry and then dusting were first on my agenda quickly followed by vacuuming. I needed to get the vacuuming done before their shows started. I worked diligently and assiduously trying my best to keep my mind off of the pain, but as soon as I started pushing that vacuum around it almost became too much to bear. I had to take frequent breaks just to breathe and keep my tears at bay. Pushing the pain to the back was not working so well with this chore, but what other choice did I have. I suffered through it constantly telling myself that I could do it and that I could lay down soon. With each searing movement I became more determined to make sure everything was spotless so the pain wouldn't get worse. Once the vacuuming was done I moved onto the bathroom; the room where I could close the door.

As soon as the door shut I slid down it completely exhausted. I just sat there thinking about how much time I was wasting and how I needed to get up. I only wanted to sit here and rest, but their voices were ringing in the back of my head while coursing through me was the pain they inflicted. I finally got up and cleaned as fast as my body would allow so I could just move onto the next area. I ran downstairs to switch the laundry and then back up to sweep and mop. After the mopping all that was left was to finish was the laundry and there was no way all of that was going to get done before bed. This is when I realized that I was set up for failure. My only hope was to get as much done as possible and hope they wouldn't be mad. I didn't have any other choice, so I started and folded laundry as quickly as the machines would allow. I thought that maybe if I sorted through the piles in the basement it would make up for the laundry not being completed. So instead of resting which I so longed to do I started going through the piles one by one. I sorted out the trash and organized the items into piles for my mother, father, and brother. This way they could easily find what they were looking for and it made the basement look better. I straightened everything up and made sure all of the piles were nice and neat, but by ten o'clock I was completely drained and only able to get to a fourth of the piles. I had finished all of the laundry except two loads and could only hope that was good enough.

With laundry in my hands I walked back up the stairs to put it away and go to bed. Maybe if I don't tell them the laundry didn't get done they won't notice and I can finish it tomorrow before they come home from work I thought. In my little 12-year-old mind this was the best plan I could come up with. The door opened with a soft creak as I feebly pushed it just far enough to slip between it and the frame. Quickly, but quietly I put all the clothes away then decided to take the chance on showering. I knew they would immediately hear the shower, but I had to make sure my open wounds were clean; at least for the moment. My shower didn't last long simply because of the pain from the water and my sheer exhaustion. All I wanted was to go to bed and forget about everything for a few hours. To close my eyes and sleep.

What I wanted and what I was going to get were two totally different things was the lesson I was soon to learn. When I opened the bathroom door they were both standing outside waiting for me. *This can only end badly. I don't think my plan is going to work. I shouldn't have taken a shower. I should have just gone to bed. At least I would have been able to lie down for a few minutes.* "Just what do you think you are doing?" said my mother in a disdainful voice. "Just who do you think you are?" she said in the same voice. "I was just taking a shower and getting ready for bed." I replied back in a tentative voice. "Did you finish everything like you were told to or did you just decide what you wanted to finish?" she asked. *And here it comes. They will find out one way or another so maybe it will be better if I just come clean now.* "I finished everything but two loads of laundry. I did go through some piles in the basement and sorted them out though while I was waiting for the laundry to finish." I said in that same tentative voice. "So instead of doing what we told you to do, you decided to go through our stuff like it's yours?" my father asked in a demanding voice. "I did do what you told me to do, but while the laundry was in the machines I thought I would organize a little. I wasn't trying to go through your stuff. Just put it in piles so you could find it easier." I said in a defensive voice. *I was only trying to make things easier for all of us. Why can't they see that?* "Who told you to go through our stuff?" bellowed my mother. "No one." I said. "So instead of finishing your chores you thought it fun to go through our stuff without permission. Well did you find anything you wanted? Find anything you wanted to keep? I know you took something! What did you take? Where is it? In your room? You know you're lucky you even have a room!" she hollered. "Maybe we should take that room away from you! You don't deserve it! You don't pay the bills around here! You walk around here like you own the place and can do whatever you want to do! You are a spoiled, ungrateful, worthless bitch! You aren't good for anything! You go through our things without asking permission and don't finish your chores! Why should you get anything?" my father howled. *I tried to finish everything. I really tried. Then I tried to clean the basement. Why can't I do anything right?*

"You answer us when we ask you a question." my mother shouted as she slapped me. My father then took me by the shoulders and shoved me into the wall as they surrounded me. My mother got right in my face and started screaming while slapping me with her hands while my father stood by and watched. I knew it was going to end this way but hoped that it wouldn't. I tried everything I could to make sure it was all done and then did more, but it didn't matter. Once my mother was done slapping me she moved out of the way so that my father could have a turn, but instead of standing in front of me he stood beside me. I then became a human ping pong ball as they shoved me back and forth while hitting me, clawing at me, spinning me, throwing me into the walls and doing whatever they wanted to do. I was so disoriented that I couldn't even put up my arms to block the blows.

Then my father shoved me while my mother tripped me then stepped out of the way as they watched me fall to the ground hitting my head. Instead of asking if I was okay or helping me get up they stood there and laughed at me. Hearing their laughs was worse than their punches or low jabs. This pierced through me because I truly understood at this moment that they didn't care about me. That they didn't love me and that I would never be loved by them again.

UNEVENTFUL

As EACH NEW day approached, I hoped that the day would
be uneventful and I could be invisible. I only wanted and
hoped to get through the day without any confrontations
or surprises. I found myself wishing away the days. I didn't
want to get out of bed and face the horror that I knew was
soon to begin. Each day came with new fears and new
anxieties that only seemed to become worse as time went
on. My days started to grow longer, more painful, more
fearful, and much more frightening. The only saving grace
I had was looking for patterns to their schemes. To try to
be one step ahead of them; to figure out their games.

My memory increasingly grew with each new lie I told
not only to my father, my mother, and my brother, but
also to everyone I came into contact with. Lying became
second nature and a means of survival. The less they knew,

the better I would be; the less they knew, the better my chances were of not being beat as ruthless and merciless. I was able to look into their eyes and lie without flinching.

With each lie, I felt as if I were stooping down to their level. I saw them lie to everyone every day in public. I had decided that I could not be like them. That I could not lie to them or anyone else. That I had to become someone different, something better, someone who didn't lie to everyone.

Taking a Closer Look

I STARTED TO look at my father, my mother, and my brother differently. I looked at the people at church differently. I looked at my friends and the teachers at school differently. I began to memorize the nuisances of every individual I came into contact with. I looked deep into their eyes when they talked to me and listened for tonality changes in the voices. I noticed the subtle looks that would pass between people and taught myself how to lipread. I became overly observant in hopes that it would help me figure out why this was happening to me. I focused all of my attention on this and applied these skills that I had honed daily into my life at "home." I thought that maybe if I could just be a fraction of a step ahead of them I could survive.

While at home I focused on these few skills I had acquired. Daily I put them to the test and learned more with each new passing day. I had now come up with a plan to get me through the agonizing pain and heartache that came with each day. I watched their hands in their fits of rage as well as their bodies. I learned how to brace myself for the impact of their punches, kicks, jabs, connects of their hands and nails against my skin, their casts of my body into the walls, and all of their interchanges and shifts as new transfers of pain were directed toward me. I knew I could not jib and jab their blows, but only stand or lay there and take them without making a sound. The only thing I could do was watch them intently and know when the next blow was coming. I was helpless but knowing when the next blow was going to come gave me something to focus on instead of the pain. Instead of wanting to scream out while the tears streamed down my face. It gave me something to hold onto until I could cry alone.

I only had one person who I could talk to. One person who knew the truth. One person I could cry to and that was Charlotte. There were many times when I saw her that tears immediately welled up in my eyes. She was the only person I could show any sort of emotion to. Charlotte was the only person who saw the nail marks and the bruises and the true pain I was in. She became the only person I could trust and lean onto. She was the very small dim light in my ever growing dark world.

Freshman Year

I HAD IT all figured out; I had a plan. I had a plan that was going to get me through until the day when I could finally get out. This great plan of mine was to just push everything as far back as I possibly could and then brace for the impact that would no doubt occur everyday.. My plan however began to crumble as my situation intensified. I was officially a nothing and a nobody in the eyes of my father and my mother. To my brother I was an annoying nothing that deserved to get every bit of it all. Not only did he cheer them on but he also united with them. They were a unified front with the main goal to cause me as much pain as they possibly could. Daily they would tell me, "You are worthless. You are a mistake and we should have never had you. You are a selfish little brat. You don't deserve a thing. You deserve to be punished for the way that you treat us. You are a lazy, useless, and incompetent person. You are unworthy of love. Nobody will ever love you. Nobody could ever love you. You will never become anything. You aren't capable of doing anything with your life. You will always be worthless." Every day I was broken down emotionally, physically, and mentally. I was constantly being pulled in every direction except for the one where I could relax and heal.

I really am worthless. I wouldn't be treated like this if I weren't and if I didn't deserve it. How could anybody love me when my own family hates me? Their words were constantly drilled into me and no matter how hard I tried to ignore them, I slowly started to believe them. Those words punctured, penetrated and pierced me deep within. Throughout the day I would hear these words repetitively and they would eat away at me. I progressively became more depressed not only by their emotional abuse, but also by their physical abuse. The physical abuse intensified and happened more often than it had any time before. There was now more force behind every hit, every throw, every tearing of my skin, and every act of physicality that they chose to inflict upon me. They began to become more cruel as time went on. As the days went on, the normalcy of the abuse began to change and became unpredictable. The predictability of the situation was the only thing that kept me going. I knew the second before I would be hit and could brace for it. I could prepare myself to be drug on the floor or to be slammed into the wall. This kept me one step ahead of them and was essential to my survival, but things were changing.

My spirit was crushed and my plan was put to shame. Nothing was the same anymore. No matter how bad it was I could always rely on knowing what was going to happen every single night; there was very little change to it. There were some nights when I would go home and everything seemed to be fine. Things seemed calm and normal. I had my regular list of chores to complete but my father and my mother would not come behind me and check to make sure everything was done to their liking. I had no idea what was going on; however, I felt a huge relief the first time this happened, but only for that first time. I went to bed without getting beat or yelled at. *For the first time I am going to get to sleep soundly! I don't have a splitting headache and I don't feel like I'm going to throw up!* These were all new things to me and I didn't know how to deal with any of it. I laid awake for about 45 minutes thinking that this couldn't actually be happening. This couldn't be real. But before long, sleep overcame me and I couldn't fight it any longer. I don't know how long I was asleep but I was awoken by a hard punch to my stomach. *There's that feeling of throwing up again.* As I doubled over because of the pain and the lack of air, I was trying to figure out what was going on. While I was lost in my thoughts another punch came barreling down and connect with my side. I immediately rolled over to protect that side, but in my response I left my other side unprotected. This became quite apparent when another punch pierced that side. So once again I rolled to protect the side that was just punched leaving the other side unprotected. I would imagine this left a little smirk on the perpetrators face because another punch came barreling down. I was stuck. Any way that I turned, left something open for a punch to contact. There was no way for me to shield myself despite my greatest efforts. I think this made the person, who by force I guessed to be my father, quite happy. I don't know how long the punching continued, but I do know I was crying through the few breaths I could take. I knew I couldn't cry loudly but I couldn't stop the tears from coming. Before I knew what was going on, my head slammed into the floor and I'm being drug into the kitchen. *This is new. Why the kitchen?* "Get up." my father said quietly almost in a whisper. *Why is he being so quiet?* I knew not to linger and question or try to figure out what was going on. As soon as I stood up he slapped me across the face. Without hesitation my hand went flying up and he caught it before it reached my face. My gaze went from his hand to his eyes as he stood there stone still squeezing my wrist tighter and tighter. He looked me straight in the eyes and told me that I was not allowed to move and if I did I would get it worse. *What?!?! What is he going to do? What is going to happen? What will happen if I move? Stand still Suzanne. Whatever happens just don't move. Don't move anything. Don't even wince. Put up the wall and just be still. Brace yourself.* I didn't know what was going to happen but I knew that I had to brace myself. I had to go further into my shell to make sure I could withstand what was going to happen. I began to change my thinking from what could happen to bracing myself

EXTRACTING SUZANNE

for the worst possible thing. I thought that if I could think about the worst outcome I could really prepare myself mentally for what would occur and hopefully it wouldn't be the worst possible thing I could think of. Then the blows started coming. The first was to my stomach and as much as I wanted to move, I wasn't about to. The next was a hard slap to my face and I just stood there. I acted as if it didn't even phase me. The next was a hard kick to my right kneecap which would have easily made me crumble to the ground, but there was no way I was going to give him that satisfaction. I just stood there as still as a statue. I didn't make a sound or give any indication that he had hurt me. I had gone to this place where he could not hurt me. Some might call this pure stubbornness, but at this moment it was pure survival. The next blows were a series of punches to the stomach followed by another kick to my leg. At this point he was getting quite aggravated and frustrated that I wasn't moving or showing any signs of being hurt. The next round was a series of slaps to my face. He went back and forth between his hands making sure my whole face was equally slapped. At the end of it I just opened my eyes and stared straight into his. I stood tall and still, not blinking as I stared at him. I could see the flames behind his eyes and I knew it was soon going to get much worse. I was more determined now than I had ever been to prove to him that I could withstand whatever he did to me. I knew to brace myself for the worse and to control my emotions so that I would stand still. Before I knew it there was a hard punch that went across my jaw. *That one hurt!*

But don't move Suzanne. Get it together because he is going to take you to your breaking point. Hold still and strong. The next was another blow to the other side of my face. *I guess he wants the bruising to be equal.* The next round was full of fast hard punches to my stomach as if I were a punching bag. It was as if he was practicing on me for an upcoming boxing match. It was becoming increasingly harder for me to stand still, but I kept thinking about his threat if I did move. It would also mean that I gave him what he wanted and I couldn't do that again. He evidently wasn't happy enough with how my face was going to bruise so he gave another two punches followed by a round of kicks to my legs. I stared him down again and wanted to give him a little smirk but I feared the outcome of that too much so I sufficed with the stare down. The next couple of rounds was a little bit of everything that went one for awhile until he had to catch his breath. As I stood there I could see he was working something up that was really going to test me. He turned and walked to the counter. When he came back he was holding a knife in his hand. I looked into his eyes and saw that there was nothing there except pure determination to make me move. Pure determination to really hurt me. My fear began to grow higher and higher. Before I didn't want to move but now I wanted to run as far away as possible but I also knew that would only make things worse. *Ok. A knife. I didn't think this would happen. This wasn't in the plan. What is he going to do? Just scare me with it or actually use it? Really a knife! Ok just calm down and stay still. Just breathe and focus on something else.....*

anything else. Stay still. Be still. Breathe. My father waved the knife right in front of my face all the while saying, "Just move. I dare you. Just move. Come on Suzanne, aren't you afraid? See what will happen if you move. Just go ahead and move." He then out of nowhere shouted "Move!" *No. Don't move. Just stand still. Don't do what he says to do. He's baiting you, just stand still. Breathe and be still.* He then took the knife and placed the tip on my arm and ran it all the way down. *What is the point of this? Is he just trying to scare me?* At that point he turned the tip just enough to pierce me. Then he ran the knife down my arm again with added pressure this time. I turned my head to see and blood started to run down. *No crying. Don't do it. No crying. Push the tears back and don't let him see. Don't show him any sign. Look away Suzanne. Go back into your shell and just stay there. Don't let him phase you no matter what.* He suddenly stopped and waved the knife in front of my face again. *Ok brace yourself for whatever is going to come next.* My father then rested the blade against my cheek. *Ok you know he's going to cut you so just be still. No movements or it will be worse and no tears.* He kept the blade resting there for awhile. It was long enough that I thought he might not cut me, but I was wrong. He then dug the blade into my cheek and pulled it down towards my lips. It was such an intense pain that I didn't know what to do. I wanted to scream and I wanted with every fiber of my being to run, but if I did, how much worse would it become. All I could do was stand there and take it. What other choice did I have? As I was standing there looking him in the eyes I didn't notice him make a fist. The next thing I heard was an intense popping sound. My eyes were watering and blood was pouring out of my nose. Then I felt this different sort of pain that I had never experienced before. I knew my nose was broken, but there was nothing I could do. Every other kid, I felt, could run to their mom or dad to help or to tell them what to do or to take them to the doctor, but my father did this to me. Who could I run to? And could I even run? Would he even let me go anytime soon? I was then told that I needed to clean up all the blood and that I needed to clean the basement tonight. He told me I was not allowed to go back to bed and if I woke anybody up much worse would happen. He stood there in front of me and told me how pathetic and stupid I was. He told me I was pathetic and was ugly with all of that blood everywhere. He said no one could ever love such an ugly person like me. Then just as soon as it started it ended as he walked away to go to bed, but not before reminding me to get to cleaning. *I think I should stay still for a little bit longer. This could be a game or a trick. Maybe he's gonna come back or maybe he really did go to bed. What is happening? Should I move? Maybe I should stay a little longer. Just stay still and listen for any signs of him coming back. Just listen.*

But nothing happened. There wasn't a sound except for my mother snoring. After several minutes, I finally decided to move. The first thing I did was clean up the blood on the floor. I figured if I got that clean and got some new clothes I could go to the bathroom downstairs to take a look at the damage.

I was shocked to see my own reflection. *He's right,* I thought, *I am ugly and there's no way anyone could love me. I can only pop this nose back in place. I don't know what else to do. I braced myself for the pure agony that was soon to occur. I put a towel in my mouth and my hands on my nose, all the while trying to talk myself into doing this.* I thought to myself just how wrong all of this was and how there was no escape. I wondered what would have happened if I had gone to bed or better yet if I just fell asleep down here. How would they even know if I did sleep a little? *Maybe I can just clean a little. Move things around a bit and then sleep a little. Now to just fix this nose.* I knew if I had any hope of getting a few minutes of sleep I needed to pop it back now and quit delaying.

As soon as I could breathe again, I got started on the hoarder of a basement. There was no cleaning that could be done. They wouldn't even notice if I did clean or if I didn't. There were boxes stacked from the floor to the ceiling with only God knows what was in them. They could have made a fortune with how many Rubbermaid tubs there were. There was fabric and sewing material everywhere and a couch that was barely visible. I didn't even know where to look much less begin. *Maybe if I just put all of the tubs together and create a walkway it will look like I did a lot....who am I kidding, that is a lot. I don't even know if that will get accomplished. Ok how about I just work on making a walkway somehow.* Now that I had some sort of idea of what to do I go to work. I started moving boxes here and there, picking up trash as I went; slowly making a trash pile. I didn't know what I was going to do with the trash besides hope there were some trash bags in the garage or empty the contents out of one box and put it all in there. Slowly throughout the night a walkway appeared. It wasn't wide and boxes were towering over you like castle walls, but at least you could walk from one end to the other. Once I cleared all of the trash out, I thought it looked much better. At least more organized and you could tell that I had done something. I only hoped that they would think I did something too. I created a little spot in the back of the room that was a safeguard for me to get a little sleep. I went and took care of my face and arm again before I took the chance to sleep. I went to my spot, moved two boxes and created the fort again. It was just big enough for me to curl up in a ball and had boxes covering the opening at the top. I left some trash over there so I could act like I was cleaning out a box if they did come downstairs. I knew if I got to sleep right away, I could get an hour in before they would start stirring. I tried to block everything out and enjoy my little safe hole. For the first time, I actually felt safe. They couldn't see me; I could hear them if they came and I knew how to get out quickly. I had everything set up. I quickly fell asleep with the peace of mind I now had, but knew I had to get up in an hour.

About an hour later I woke up and a smile quickly came over my face. I knew I was still safe. All I wanted was to keep this feeling. To remain in my safe spot; to remain hidden, but soon the dread of know what was lying ahead hit me. I knew that I must get out before my spot was discovered and that too was taken away. Everything else was and this would be no different. So I crawled out and attempted to stretch. The attempt was pure agony. It did not go over so well. I was stiff and I was so sore. I knew my face would look awful and had no idea how I was going to cover that up. The best I could do was make up and a bandage. I knew I would have to put the bandage in such a way that I could use a cover up story easily without getting too many questions. I moved a few more boxes around just so that it would sound like I was still working in case they were listening. I made my way to the mirror in the bathroom and willed myself to look. I knew I had to look as bad as I felt, but when I looked it was much worse than I thought it would be.

Is this even me? Could this be me? He really did a number on me last night. There's no way I can cover all of this up. I now know why icing is so important. My face was swollen up to double its regular size. There was a huge gash going from the top of my cheek bone to just above my lip. My face was all sorts of colors. From black to blue to red to ghost white. My eyes were sunken in with dark circles under them. My arm did not look any better and I didn't dare look at my abdomen. My knees were both so swollen that it felt like I would fall at any moment. *How am I going to cover this up? If I don't come up with a good story I know it will only get worse. Think Suzanne! Think! You can't take another night like this again! Maybe they'll let me stay home. Afterall, he did come after my face. I now won't look like the perfect little daughter and that would mess up their appearance that they have worked so hard to maintain. Think of a story Suzanne!* I came up with absolutely nothing. What could even been said happened besides the truth? There is no way to hide this one. If anyone took one look at me they would know exactly what had happened. They would have instantly saw that I was beat up last night. I can't hide this one. *I really don't want to have to deal with the looks and the questioning glances as I try to cover for them. But I also don't want to stay here. God knows what will happen if they have me stay home, but God knows what would happen if I didn't cover for them well enough. There is no way out of this. I am right where they want me to be.*

I went back to cleaning because I had nothing else to do. I didn't dare go upstairs until they called me. I knew better. I started putting boxes together that had some of the same stuff but maintained my wall so they walkway would still be visible. Before long, I heard someone walking down the stairs. I figured by the speed, it was my father, but I didn't turn until I heard my name. There it was in a low raspy voice and my fears were true. I had to face the man that had done this to me. I took my time turning around. I'm not sure why other than the fact that I didn't want to see him. He stared into my eyes for a few moments before he started looking me up and down. It was like he was admiring how banged up I was. He seemed to be looking for any spot that he missed, but I don't know how he could find one. When he was done admiring he said, "If only you could be a good girl you wouldn't get punished." I had no idea how to respond to that so I just remained still and quiet. He then said, "Well it's a good thing you aren't going to school today because it doesn't look like you did anything down here." *Well I won't have to deal with everyone else, but now I'm stuck here all day. The one place I long to be away from.* "Did you even do anything when I sent you down here? This place looks horrible! You are so lazy! Why can't you be more like your brother? He is responsible; he is respectful and a lot more fun to be around. Why can't you be like him? I had better be able to see that you actually did what you were told to do by the time I come back or you will have another night like last night, but this time I guarantee that you will move!" He was calm and quiet. I have learned to fear him more when he is like that. If I don't do everything, and I do mean everything, exactly the way he wants it, then he really will go through with his threats. What will he do to guarantee my moving? What could be worse than what he already did? *He wasn't even remorseful. He wasn't shocked with how I looked. In fact, he seemed pleased with himself. What happened to him? I used to be his little girl. The little girl he would sing to sleep at night. I was perfect in his eyes. Why aren't I anymore? What is so wrong with me? What have I done so wrong? I guess he's right...if I were more like my brother, they would like me more. They adore him and he can do no wrong. Why can't I just be more like him so all of this will stop? Everything would be fine if I could just be more like him. Why can't they love me anymore? What have I done? How have I caused all of this? Why can't I just be what they want me to be?*

I was back to cleaning soon enough. The only thing I could think to do was to organize the boxes some more into categories. At least this way it would be easier for them to find their stuff. I still wanted to keep the walkway and was desperate to keep the safe hole I had created. I found a marker and tape and started labeling everything as best as I could. I was fearful of going through their stuff too much and I didn't dare throw anything away. I knew those were two lines that I could not cross no matter what. Once I knew everyone was out of the house I turned on some music and just kept my head down working away. My only hope was that they could see that I had done something; that I had been working. I was able to condense some boxes down as I went and thought that I should start some laundry. Maybe I could get some bonus points if I completed the laundry that was down here. I will most likely still get beat, but maybe not as bad this way. Around lunch time, my father came home to check on what I was doing. I prayed that he could see a difference. When he came down, I decided that if I were overly nice and bubbly maybe his mood would change too. "Hey, dad! I washed some of the clothes. You have some of your dress shirts hanging up to dry right now and I just started a load of pants. I have been labeling all of the boxes and putting them together so that it's easier for us to find stuff down here. Like over there are all of the tubs of pictures. Here, right in front, are all of the Beanie Babies. Over there by the piano is all of the music. Your records, atracs, and cassette tapes. Also the piano music is in a box on the other side of the piano. I still need to go through everything in the back, but I've made progress." I only hoped he would be pleased and didn't come home for a stress relieving session. He finally said, "Looks like you've been working. It's looking good. Why don't you come up for some lunch?" I felt a huge sense of relief. I turned to go upstairs with him not even thinking if he would do anything. He seemed like he was in a good mood and instead of worrying about everything, I was going to try to take it for what it was worth. I was just going to be happy and be a normal kid eating lunch with their father. The bad would soon enough happen, but times like this were few and far between. I had to enjoy it and had to hope that someday my dad would come back. Maybe that day could be today.

We made sandwiches together and all I could think about was why everyday couldn't be like this. He was in a good mood. He was smiling and laughing and actually looked like he loved me. His eyes looked inviting instead of hostile and I wanted more than anything to just be loved by him. We talked about what big story he was working on at the paper and when the deadline was. We talked about my grandma and when we were going to see her next and how she was doing. We talked about what was going on at church and if there were any youth events coming up. It was normal, it was comfortable, it was refreshing, it was more than I could have imagined would happen. It restored my hope in them changing. It restored my desire to be close to them and to gain their love again. I wanted to find some way where that was possible. Someway where he could look at me with love in his eyes all the time. Someway where my mother could give me a hug and I wouldn't shudder. Someway where I was their daughter in their eyes once again. This lunch was more than I could have asked for. I felt like a normal kid for once. A normal kid who didn't have to hide anything. A normal kid whose parents loved her and a kid who wasn't afraid to come home. I had to do everything I possibly could to keep things like this. I didn't want to live in fear anymore. I wanted things to stay like this, so I knew I had to do everything perfectly for awhile.

Once he left, I went back downstairs to finish the laundry and cleaning. I figured if he was happy about it earlier, he would be even happier if I finished it. I had no other goal other than to show him that I had accomplished what he told me to do. By the time he got home, I wanted everything to be done. I wanted to show it off to him and for him to be proud of me. I wanted to see that look in his eyes when he looked at me, at least one more time.

When he came home, I had all of the laundry done and the basement was completed. Every box and tub were labeled and put into categories. There was a clear walkway and I managed to keep my secret hiding spot. All of the trash was gone and it was easy to tell where things were. I was even able to make the couch visible with enough room around it for you to sit down and relax if you wanted to. I thought there was a complete and drastic change.

Like night from day; now if only he thought there was a change. If only he could tell; I could see that look again. I could be his daughter again. He could love me once more and be proud of me behind these closed doors. I couldn't wait to show it to him. I heard him coming down the stairs and I became excited and nervous. I knew if he didn't like it, I would be in a whole lot of trouble, but if he did like it....oh if he did like it, I could be loved. When he came to the doorway, I went over to meet him. I wanted to walk him around so that he could see where everything was and all that I had done. I didn't want him to miss anything. My goal was to make everything as easily accessible as possible so that a trip down here would only take a few minutes. He seemed interested in where everything was and even asked questions as to where things were. My spirits were high and I knew this was going well. *I've finally done something right. Tonight will be a good night.* Once the tour was over he told me that I had done a good job and he was impressed with how well organized everything was. He even gave me a hug and said, "Thank you. This is what we expect from you every single time. Do you think you can do that? Do you think you can quit misbehaving and just obey?" I replied with, "I can dad." With that, we walked back upstairs and my mother was there waiting. My father told her that I had done a great job and had earned my keep today. She looked from him to me and then said, "Ok." It was as if she was routing for me to do a bad job. Like she was not happy with my father's answer and I immediately went back to being that fearful child. I could no longer embrace the goodness of what had happened today after the horrible night. I could only stare at her in disbelief. Just like that she had crushed all of the hope I had gained throughout the day. My smile faded and my shoulders slumped. I knew this was what she wanted, but I couldn't help it. She hadn't seen what my father had done to me yet, and she barely even looked at me. She didn't come to my aid and yell at my father. She didn't scoop me up in her arms and protect me. No. She did the complete opposite and crushed my spirit. She just completely dismissed me. I had hoped that she would at least show a little shock in her face when she saw me, but I guess that was hoping for too much. She just turned away to get to her chair.

Does this mean the rest of the night is going to be bad? Didn't I do a good job? Even my father had said that I did, so why can't she acknowledge that? Why can't she see that I am doing my best? I decided it best to make my presence sparse and try to remember the good that had happened today. I went to my room to do some writing. I wanted to remember when my father loved me and was proud of me. I didn't ever want to forget it. I had to capture it. Slowly throughout the writing, I found that hope again. I found that little thread that I could hold onto. I came out for dinner and after doing the dishes, I was able to go to bed. I was exhausted and sore and for once was thankful that tomorrow was Saturday. That night I prayed for my father and my mother to sleep the whole night and late into the morning. I prayed that my wounds would heal and that

I wouldn't be as sore the next day. I prayed for a restful night and for some much needed sleep. Before I knew it, it was morning. *Did I really just sleep the whole night? Did they not come wake me up? Are they even awake?* I intently listened for them but heard nothing. I slowly got up, not knowing what to do. It had been so long since this had happened. I just didn't want to wake them up. If they were still sleeping that meant I could have a few minutes to myself....in peace. I didn't have to worry about them barging in or dragging me out of bed. I could just stand up when they came. In a way, I felt secure knowing I would know when they came. I wrote for a little bit, as writing had become the thing that kept me stable. It was a way for me to release my feelings; the feelings I was not allowed to have with them. It was a way for me to document what happened and it made me feel in control. This was one thing I could do and hide from them. They couldn't take this away from me. I just had to be careful. When I was done writing, I picked up a book. I could not believe they were still in bed and I had this time to myself. It was a rare treat and I soaked up every second of it. I had to make the most of this time and I did so by lying in bed; one of the things I didn't get to do very often.

Reading was one of my favorite things to do. It allowed me to escape my world and go someplace else. It allowed me to live through the lives of the characters in the books. I was able to be a kid with an imagination when I journeyed into these great stories. The fear and the worry that continually consumed me disappeared when I could dive into a book. It didn't matter if I was able to read a paragraph or the whole book, it always calmed me. Books allowed me to see that there was something better out there. That life was good outside of these four walls. The stories filled me with and I knew if I could only survive, things would be better. These books gave me the thread of hope that I could hold onto.

Soon enough everyone was stirring about and I knew my day would soon begin. I didn't know what kind of day it would be. Would it be full of pleasant surprises or would it be a day filled with beatings? Would it be a day where I felt loved or where I felt despised by all in the house? I could only hang onto the hope of surviving and moving e forward to another day. One day at a time was sometimes too big of a goal. Sometimes surviving one second at a time was the goal at hand. I hoped this could be a day-at-a-time goal and not a second-at-a-time goal. My father opened my door and was surprised to see me awake. "Hey, how long have you been awake?" He asked. "I've been up for almost two hours probably." "Have you just been here the whole time?" He asked. "I didn't want to wake anybody so I just stayed in here." I replied. With that, he turned and left. I just stayed in my room not quite sure of what he wanted. Was he mad that I hadn't done anything? Was it good that I didn't wake them up? I figured I would find out soon enough, but nothing happened. Nothing. No one else came in my room. No one else knocked. Everyone left me alone. *What is going on? Is everyone sick?* I was able to come and go as I pleased. No one yelled at me or hit me. In fact, no one even talked to me, but that was fine with me. I liked this much better! I spent most of the day in my room reading or just laying on my bed. I looked out the window for a little bit and just watched. Everything was quiet and it was the most relaxed I had felt in a long time.

The next several weeks remained much the same. Nothing big happened. My mother seemed to soften and became more inviting. She would say hi to me on most days and would actually ask me about my day. Nobody really yelled at me or hit me. Most nights I was able to sleep. I became more relaxed and slowly let my walls down. I didn't second guess them, but instead took everything as it was. I was just happy they wanted to talk to me, weren't yelling at me all the time, and weren't beating me. I was becoming more comfortable and began to feel like a part of their family again. Things were changing. What I dreamed of, what I prayed for, was finally coming true. I truly couldn't believe it. I was having a hard time wrapping my mind around what was happening. My eyes were seeing one thing, but my mind wasn't able to process it as reality.

Things had truly changed; my life was wonderful, until I had taken all of my walls down. Everything was beyond words, and then, it happened. Without a warning, without a sign, the beatings started up again. The mother that I had grown to know went back to being the terror I was afraid of. My entire world completed shattered. My heart was broken beyond repair. How could this happen? How could I have let them in and trusted them? How could I have given myself over to them and felt like such a part of their lives only for it all to be taken away in a moment's notice? How did this happen? All I wanted was for my mother to be back. For my dad to be back, but now they have disappeared again. Somehow everything changed. I was completely devastated and didn't know what to do. I couldn't comprehend what was happening much less come up with some way to deal with it. How would I ever get through this? I thought it was all over. I continually questioned what I did to cause this. How could I have caused such extreme hatred?

This time things didn't go back to the bad that they were before, but they got worse. My life took a steep turn downhill and there was no way back up. I kept getting pushed farther and farther down until I had nowhere to go. This is exactly where they wanted me to be, I had realized. They wanted me so far down, that nothing and nobody could get me back up. The beatings became harder, more frequent and lasted much longer. The sleepless nights went from a few every week to almost every night. I was lucky to get a couple hours of sleep every night and many nights I only got a few minutes. None of this bothered me as much as the dramatic shift in our relationship. We went from something good to something completely and totally horrible once again. If they were hoping to crush me with this, they most certainly did.

EVERYTHING TURNED BLACK

WITH EACH PASSING day the light grew dimmer and dimmer until I was eventually left in complete darkness.. I saw no way out of this hole they had buried me in. The more I tried to find a way, the deeper in the hole I went. Every attempt was futile and it soon became apparent that I would never get out of this. I would be stuck forever; I was truly trapped. I finally realized that there was only one way out. There was only one way out and only one way to end all of the pain. I knew there was only one way, in which I thought, I could get some rest. I knew there was only one way to end it all. I was so broken, that I thought this would solve everything.

I began to plot out ways to end it all. I thought about taking pills. Really between my father and my mother we had the whole pharmacy at the house. Any one of their pills would do the trick. I then thought about starving myself, cutting, and finally hanging myself. I actually thought about ending it all for a good while before I decided to give it a try. The first attempt were the pills, but both my mother's and my father's prescriptions were being filled so I decided to take a lot of Tylenol instead. As the time passed and nothing happened, I realized I hadn't taken enough. All that was occurring was an upset stomach and I was a little tired. *I can't even kill myself correctly,* I thought. *This should be easy. Take enough pills and then you'll drift off…what's so difficult about this?* Once nothing happened, I just gave up on taking anymore. I was disappointed that this plan didn't work. I had hyped myself up for this to be the end and I was honestly okay with it. I believed with all of my being that this would finally end it once and for all. I just walked back to my room not believing I was still alive.

In the meantime I stopped eating as much. In fact I barely ate anything. I thought if I can't kill myself with pills, I can at least slowly stare myself. I finally decided to try it again, but this time I would do it differently. This time I would cut myself, but I knew I had to hide it. I really just wanted to see what it would feel like before I fully went through with it. I knew I couldn't cut my wrists because too many people would see it. The next best place would be on my upper thighs. Even with my shorts, no one would see it, if I cut high enough. So one night, I gave it a go. It was a weird sensation. It hurt, but it also felt good. It was actually a welcome change. For the first time in a long time I felt something. I was in control. If I wanted to make it hurt worse all I had to do was press down harder. Some cuts were deeper than others, but it wasn't anything that would cause a lot of harm. When I stopped, I wanted to start it back up again. I had never been in control of anything and now I was addicted. The pain fed me that immediate feedback that I was looking for. Every cut allowed a sigh of relief to run through me. It was like anything else I had ever imagined. By the time I had finished, my thighs were nothing more than bloody red stripes. Not only did the pain from the cutting create a sensation, so did seeing the marks I had created. For some reason I became addicted to this and instead of using it as a means to kill myself, I used it as a means to gain some input. I used it as something that allowed me to be in control. I used it as a release.

Now that I knew this wasn't going to be the way I killed myself, the only other option was strangulation. This was my last hope at ending this nightmare, also known as, my life. I wasn't quite sure how I could do this. After thinking for awhile I thought of using my sheet and tie it to my bed. I had a daybed at this point with white decorative metal. It was decently sturdy. Enough to hold my weight at least. I thought if I tied the sheet short enough I could just dangle myself off the side. I didn't really know what to do. I tried this on multiple occasions, but each time I would just black out and then come to again. I would change the rope, I would tie it somewhere else, I would move while I dangled, but still nothing worked.

While still attempting strangulation, I made the decision to talk to a few of my friends about what they thought about suicide. I just wanted to know hypothetically if I would ever be missed. I wanted to know how they would react and if they thought there was anything wrong with ending your life. I was increasingly becoming more and more frustrated that I kept coming back after every black out. All I wanted was for all of this to end once and for all. I did not think that was much to ask for, but apparently, that, along with everything else was just exactly that.

One of the friends put two and two together. She figured out that I had been attempting to kill myself and told the school counselor. I got called to the counselors office where she proceeded to ask me a serious of questions. I knew the second I was called to go there I had been ratted out. I knew one of those "friends'" of mine had told and now I had to come clean. This was the last thing that I wanted to happen. I wished at that very moment that I had been successful any of those other times. I figured what more do I have to lose? I would get beat, there would probably be some new game that I would have to play, I would be screamed at, I would be called degrading things….what else of me was there to lose? My father and my mother had control over everything and I knew without a shadow of a doubt that I meant nothing to them. All they wanted me for was to relieve their stress. I wouldn't gain anything from telling the counselor everything and I wouldn't lose anything either.

I proceeded to tell the counselor how many suicide

attempts I had made as well as what I had tried. When she asked me why, I knew I couldn't tell. I knew that was one line I could not cross, so I simply said, "I'm just not a happy kid." She wasn't pleased with this answer, but I had no other choice. That was the only answer I was going to give her. She told me she would have to call in my father and we would all have to discuss what has been happening. I didn't plead for her not to call him, I didn't spill my guts to her, I just said, "Ok." From the second I was called to her office; I knew she would have to call him and I knew the show he was going to put on. When he arrived, he did not disappoint. He wrapped me up in his arms, kept telling me he loved me, and just kept asking why through the tears. Even though I knew this was how he would react, it infuriated me beyond words. He was the reason I was here. He was the reason I tried to kill myself over and over and over again. He was the reason why I hated my life. He was the reason why I never wanted to see the blue sky again. He was the reason for it all. He finally sat in the chair next to me and just asked, "Suzanne, why do you want to kill yourself? Why have you tried this?" I was so livid with this show that I looked him straight in his eyes and said, "You know exactly why." I held my gaze until he looked away. I knew before I said it, I shouldn't have. I knew I would get beat harder than any other time, but I didn't care anymore. I was so mad at my friend for telling, for not being able to kill myself, for the way my father had just acted, and for the very reason why I was here. Something inside me had just snapped and I couldn't stay quiet any longer. He turned to look back at me and said, I will take her home with me and I'll keep an eye on her. *Nice recovery. Great way to cover that up. If people only knew who you truly are. If people could just glimpse inside our windows every once in a while they would see that you are far from what you pretend to be. I don't even care that I'm getting beat for this one. At least it's one that I deserve. One where I know I blatantly disobeyed. Go ahead and do your worst. I'm fully prepared. Take that knife on me again. With any luck you'll get carried away and kill me yourself. Then this will all be over for me and for once people will see you for who you truly are.* My father didn't take me home but took me to get some food to go and we met my mother during her lunch break at her school where she was working. I was so completely confused by all of this but I also knew better than to say anything. I sat in the car silently looking out the window until we got the school. Once at the school, I hesitated to get out of the car. I was no longer angry, but ashamed and confused. Ashamed I had attempted suicide several times. Ashamed I wasn't successful. Ashamed my friend told. Ashamed that now people in charge at school knew something that intimate about me. But as much as I was ashamed I was just as much confused as to what was happening. I knew my mother didn't know why we were there and I didn't know what to say. My father ended up telling her so I didn't have to. My parents seemed to be in a state of shock and for once actually concerned. I was then told that it was mandated for me to receive counseling services and that we would be going as a family. Just the three of us. Now this thought made my anxiety skyrocket. I couldn't imagine being back in a counselors office after 5th grade. They didn't believe me then and they still don't believe what I said. I argued with them about going to therapy and how it wasn't needed. None of my arguments were successful and we eventually went to a therapist of their choice in Joplin, Missouri.

Counseling

THE DRIVE TO Joplin is only about 20 minutes but that ride seemed to last forever and go by as quickly as the blink of an eye at the same time. *I can't go back to a counselor. Not after what happened last time. And now I'm supposed to go with them? I was warned to not say anything to anybody. If I lie I'm going to be in trouble and if I tell the truth I'm going to be in trouble. What am I going to do? I know staying silent isn't going to be an option. Either way I am in trouble.* The ride over there was filled with silence and anxiety. Before I knew it we were there and I had decided that I would just spill the beans to the therapist. Just tell whoever it was all that had and was happening. We went into her office and she had me sit in between my parents on a loveseat. Now talk about being uncomfortable in just about every way imaginable, but this was my chance. If therapy was mandated due to the suicide attempts, I might as well explain why I was so adamant about killing myself. I don't remember much of the therapy session other than spilling my guts. Once I was done talking the therapist looked me dead in the eyes and said, "You are a liar. I know your parents and how good they are. Your father is the editor of the newspaper and an upstanding individual. Your mother is a special education teacher. She has a heart of gold. They would never do anything like what you are talking about. You are a liar and just want attention." I felt so completely defeated. I knew I was going to get beat to a bloody pulp no matter what, but I thought it was worth the risk in hopes of the therapist believing me, but now all that hope was gone. Now I had to anticipate the beating on the way home. I knew it was going to be bad, just didn't know how bad.

THE AFTERMATH

I KNEW I was in for it when we pulled into the driveway and they both looked at each other and smirked then looked at me. "Get out of the car and get into the living room" my father said. I knew better than to argue or make a sound. I got out as quickly as I could and with my head hung low I walked into the living room. I didn't even sit down because I wasn't told I was able to. I just stood there looking down at the carpet and how I didn't get it spotless the night before. When they walked in, I didn't even look up. I knew I was in more trouble than I had ever been before. I knew there was nothing I could do but to take it and pray I make it out alive. *God, please help me. God help me survive. Help m…..* and that was the end of my prayer because the blows started. They were on both sides of me just like they were in the counselors office. There was no escape. There was only pain. Deep, intense pain. I fell to the ground after both of my knees were kicked so many times, I couldn't hold myself up anymore. Once on the ground a belt was being swished through the air at lightning speed. I was hit from my head to my toes with that belt more times than I could possibly count. The welts were immediate and it felt like my whole body was on fire. A fire like Hell that you can't escape. *Oh please stop! I can't take this anymore! Oh finally he stopped.* When I thought the belt was over, I was rolled over to my other side and my shirt torn off. *Why is he tearing off my shirt? I know that can only mean one thing. Please no, no, no, no, no. NOOOOO!!!!* Soon the belt was swishing through the air and landing with such intensity. No matter how I turned that belt never relented. I couldn't keep the tears in and this only made the belt come down harder. *Suzanne just stop crying and it will end. Suck it up. This is what you get for telling. He told me not to tell.* My body was covered in welts. Welts deep enough you could see every detail of the belt on me. I thought that was the worst of it, but I was far from wrong. I was then lifted up and there were my father's hands around my throat pushing me against the wall. He took one hand off of my throat and with the other began to punch me as hard as he could in my stomach. Then my mother would come in and slap my face repeatedly in between blows. With each punch, his hand around my neck squeezed tighter and with each slap to the face the harder it was to breathe. It felt like my eyes were bulging out of my head from the pressure but I was as helpless as could be. As I was passing out there was a hard punch, no doubt given by my father, to my face and then he let go. I instantly knew my nose was broken….again. I assume he let go so quickly so he didn't get my blood on him. *Damn it God, you could do something! Make this stop! Make it stop now!!!* The pain was so horrible. It was different than last time my nose was broken. This punch felt like I should have been flying through the wall. When my father let go I collapsed to the ground gasping for breath. My throat was on fire. I couldn't swallow. I couldn't breathe. I couldn't see straight but could only see blurry spots. I had no idea where the next blows were coming from except that they were unrelenting. *I am about to throw up, but there is no way that I can. If I throw up, it will just make everything even worse than it is now. Keep it in Suzanne. Try to breathe through it. I can't do this anymore. I can't….* I tried to turn away as best as I could, but I only had so much room when I was shoved up against the wall. When I threw up, my parents laughed at me. I think this hurt more than the blows. Here I am, their daughter, on the floor in agony, with a broken nose, welts all over me, broken ribs, blood pouring out, and just threw up, and they are looking down at me laughing. They were happy with what they have done and thought it was hysterical that I was in such pain. I thought it would end with them laughing at me but once again I was wrong. They continued to kick me. They would take turns all the while telling me that I am a liar. Telling me they are the best people in the world. Telling me I only want attention and they are doing just that….giving me attention. I was then drug around the living room by my hair. *Carpet burn on welts. OUCH!!! Stop!!* I was grabbing at my hair to ease some pain because I clearly couldn't stop the carpet burns. *Please! Just! Stop! Stop! I can't handle anything else. Stop!!!!* I don't know how long they drug me around the carpet but it ended up with that damn nail again. If I thought there was blood before with my nose, there was about to be so much more now. I didn't have anything to soak up the blood that continued to pour from my nose or to catch the blood from my back now. *I swear that make sure that nail is up before they start beating me. One of these days I'm going to drag them over it and laugh at them. DAMN IT!!!! As if things weren't bad enough they have to add the nail to it! Why won't they just stop? I know I talked to the counselor but just stop already! I learned my lesson….don't talk. Now just stop!!* But of course they didn't. They just continued and went on for what seemed like hours. While I was laying lifeless on the floor when they stopped dragging me over the nail, they began to kick me again and stomp on my stomach. Then the belt came out once again. If there wasn't a centimeter covered in welts, there for sure wasn't one part of me that wasn't untouched now. I was then thrown around the room more times than I could count. I had to fight staying awake. The sheer amount of pain I was in was unlike anything I had ever experienced. There was no way for me to brace for anything. There was no way to know what was coming next. I was choked more times that I could count, punched more times than is humanly possible, kicked to where too many ribs were broken than I could count, and was a bloody, broken mess. To add insult to injury, I was thrown down the stairs. I don't mean just pushed, but I mean picked up and thrown. I was then told to get back up the stairs and under a time limit. *Oh My GOD!!! Everything is broken! Nothing works anymore. How am I supposed to get back up those stairs within his time limit? Just get up Suzanne. Push the pain aside. Just get back up.* I didn't make it back up the stairs within his time limit. It just wasn't possible. This sequence happened several more times. The last time I crawled my way back up the stairs, I collapsed on the floor. They just shouted at me saying that I was a liar and this is what happens to liars. They said they were making sure I regretted failing at suicide. "I bet you wish you were dead now." "You are such a failure, you couldn't even kill yourself." "You wanted attention, well looks like you got some." After that, they left me laying on the ground unable to move. I felt as if everything in my body was broken. My brain said to get to my room, but my body just screamed an unwillingness to move. I felt my parents looking back at me and just smiling but I couldn't be for sure. *Come on Suzanne, get up. No don't get up, just crawl to your room. It's not that far. Just move one leg, one arm. Baby steps. Come on Suzanne. You can do it. Just get to the room.* Once I finally inched my way to my room, I completely collapsed.

THERAPY

THE NEXT SEVERAL months we continued to go to therapy, but I remained silent. I didn't utter a single sound. I was too afraid to say anything that may come back to make things worse. We then stopped seeing the woman and they took me to see another counselor. This time it was a man. *Seriously?! They just don't stop do they? There is absolutely no way that I am talking to him.* Now this was a whole new kind of anxiety associated with counseling considering what happened in 5th grade. These therapy sessions were much different because I went in by myself. The therapist shut the door and locked it behind him. He then had me sit on his couch with all the blinds closed. There were several times he wanted me to close my eyes while on the couch. There was no way in Hell I was going to do that. I remember crying and pleading every week when we had to go to Joplin for my appointment. The crying and pleading did absolutely nothing to stop my parents from taking me. During each session I became mute and disobedient. I didn't utter a sound nor did I do anything the therapist told me to do. These therapy sessions became a waste of time and a source of extreme anxiety for me.

SILENCE

NEEDLESS TO SAY, I didn't gain anything from therapy. After the first session where I barely made it out alive, I didn't dare say anything again especially to people I knew my parents had a connection with. For the next several months, I stayed silent. I deeply felt what happened the one time I talked, but the abuse never stopped, just my voice. I became a shell of a person. In fact the only time I really talked was when I was playing sports and even at that I didn't feel as if I were any good. My self-esteem was as low as low could go and I knew I was completely helpless. My situation was hopeless. I wanted to kill myself every second of every day, but I made a promise to a dear friend, that I wouldn't attempt again. I also knew if the school found out, I would have to get right back on this merry-go-round of counseling again. Nothing good was happening in my life. My life was nothing but dark. The darkness didn't go away and the anger in me grew stronger and stronger. I didn't understand my life. My life didn't have purpose except to be the human punching bag for my "family".

SPORTS

THE ONE THING I could count on, was for my parents to be at my games. And not to just be regular fans, but to be over-the-top fans. The fans that get technicals and we end up losing the game. My father was so loud in the stands, but my teammates for whatever reason loved his "Yip-Yip" cheer. I, on the other hand, hated it. As the years went by, I grew to hate/love it. It was such a show put on. A public façade to make sure no one would ever believe me. I grew to love it, because, for once they were invested in me. It was the only time they supported me even if it was just for a show. I knew better than to show any signs of hatred. I had to play along with my teammates in their love for his cheering. I had to join in on the public façade as well. We always lived a double life, but now it was intensified. The one thing in my life I was good at was sports. They became my sole outlet to the anger, anxiety and depression. The volleyball became the faces of my parents and my brother with each serve and spike. The girl elbowing me on the basketball court ended up getting the wrath of my elbows right back. Sports also became a cover up for all of the bruises, scratches, limping, headaches, tiredness, broken body parts, etc. It was an easy lie and one everyone believed. It always bothered me how easy it was for them to come up with lies, but there was no way I was giving up sports. That is until I had to give up basketball. The beatings got so bad and so often that something had to give.

New/Old Punishment

BREATHING GOT MORE and more difficult as the years passed. It could have been for a number of reasons but for one I believe to be the primary reason was the intensity of taking an old punishment and making it new again. This became a fun go-to for them, but such a nightmare for me. They would take a mixture of chemicals, any cleaning chemicals and beyond and put them in the bathroom. They would dump them out then lock the sole air vent (the one time I opened it, they caught me, and well, that ended horribly). They would lock the bathroom door and then cover the door draft with whatever they wanted to. The mixture of the chemicals would become toxically suffocating. The fog from the mixture of chemicals would fill my lungs causing me to gasp for my next breath. Each breath hurt beyond anything I could ever possibly describe. I would begin having coughing fits which only made everything hurt more, but it wasn't something that could be helped. Depending on my parents mood, I could be in there for a little bit or for an extended period of time. I felt as if I were slowly suffocating but I was completely and totally helpless. I would much rather get beat than to endure this. With each second that ticked by, I knew it was a second closer to my death. I would cough up blood each time. All I could do was pray that they would unlock the door to let me out of this horrible deathtrap. I would be collapsed on the floor just praying to make it through.

This was an old punishment that the began to use more and more often. I think this took a drastic toll on my overall health. This kind of punishment made it very difficult for me to breathe on a daily basis. During basketball season, this kind of punishment intensified until I was eventually hospitalized. The mixture of anxiety, not sleeping, the daily and constant beatings and the chemical punishments sent my body into a complete shut-down. The doctors told me to say my good-byes. This was the moment I knew my family was finally getting what they wanted. I knew I wasn't wanted, but I also knew they wanted the attention of me being sick and my death. I knew they would put on a show and have everyone feeling sorry for them. Weeks passed and my body began to heal but my spirit in no way had. I had come to terms with death. It was afterall what I had tried to do just a short while ago to stop all of the pain. Just because my body was healing, breathing was still a constant struggle and because of this I had to eventually quit playing basketball. My heart was completely broken. My spirit was shattered. Sports were my safe haven and my only release. My parents had almost killed me and no, I wasn't dead, but a part of me died when I had to quit basketball. My parents were experts at not getting caught and taking away everything I loved.

THE NEXT FEW YEARS

THE NEXT FEW years were much the same with a few changes. Food was used as a punishment, but more specifically the complete lack of food. I was no longer allowed to eat and was forced to throw up every day after school. This was a whole new level of torment and one my barely holding on body wasn't prepared for. By this point I had gotten used to constantly being sick but I wasn't used to being continually hungry. The psychological torment increased over the years. But there was still this desire in me to please them. I thought if I could just do something right, just one time, I could gain their love. I thought if I could figure out a way to be more like my brother, then just maybe, they would love me too.

"You are absolutely worthless." "You are so incredibly ugly." "There is no way anyone could possibly love you;

I know I don't." "I want to throw up every time I see you or think about you." "You can't do anything right." "Why can't you be more like your brother?" "Why do you always cause so much trouble?" "Why are you so worthless?" "You are the biggest mistake of our lives." "I wish you would just die already." "You are a piece of shit." "You are lower than a piece of shit." "You will never amount to anything." "You are a nobody." "You are a nothing." After you are told these things every day during beatings, during errands, during life, you believe them. Afterall these are the people who are supposed to love you the most and protect you the most. I had absolutely no self-esteem. I truly believed everything they were saying about me.

I had learned that in order for anyone to believe me, I would need picture proof. I was told the bruises and marks on my body were not enough. I saved up all of my money to buy a disposable camera in order to take pictures. I had just gotten the pictured developed when my parents found them in my room. When I walked in, I believed with all of me that I was going to die. The rage I witnessed in their eyes is only something you can experience and to this day I can see that look. As I stood there, frozen, I watched them come towards me in slow motion. *Here it comes. Here is when I die. God just make it quick.* When they reached me there was no way I could anticipate the sheer force with which I was hit. My head was banging on anything and everything with each blow. There was no way to try to control my body at all. I was thrown across the room more times that I could possibly count. I was already blacking out from the pain. Somewhere during all of this, the knife came out. *Just stab me and get it over with.* My father held me against the wall by my throat squeezing tighter and tighter but he didn't have the knife in his hand. My mother had the knife. She held that knife to my face and pushed in, then ran it up and down my arms cutting them open. She then went to my legs and cut my pants until she could get to my bare legs. That knife was cutting in deeper and deeper. As the knife was cutting, it became harder and harder to do anything. All I could feel was the knife and his hands squeezing around my neck. I don't know what happened next but when I came to, I was on the floor with my father holding the knife over me. He was the one doing the cutting and digging now while my mother just watched. I knew better than to move or make a sound. *Oh God, why didn't you just let them kill me?! Then the pain would all go away! Let me DIE!!! Or make them stop! Oh please stop! Please, please, please, please!!!!* Then I was kicked hard on my head several times but that's not at all where the kicking ended. More ribs were broken along with my nose. I felt like a human punching bag and pin cushion. The blows didn't stop and neither did the yelling and laughing. This time the nail wasn't enough for them. They drug me over that nail while pushing the knife into my stomach and chest. I was gashed open from my head to my toes. Silent tears streamed down my face but nothing changed. When they were finished with the nail they drug me down to the bathroom and I knew what was coming next. The only solace I found in this was that I would be alone. I don't know how long I was in the bathroom, but I know I don't remember coming out. I woke up to being punched and my father banging my head on the floor repeatedly. I knew now, that they didn't intend to kill me, they just wanted me almost dead. They wanted me to feel everything they were doing to me. Next thing I know they were beating me with anything they could get their hands on. Belts, cords, rulers, shoes, spatulas, etc. I had nothing on at this point. Nothing to take at least a little of the blows. Nothing to shield me. I would try to cover but that only made the blows so much worse. It wasn't like they were even taking turns, they were going all out at the same time. Instantly welts formed and bruises emerged. Instantly my skin (the part that wasn't cut up) was torn apart and bleeding. I didn't think there was anything else they could do, but they found something because the abuse didn't end there. The abuse continued and continued without ceasing. They had to take breaks in between the beating but that didn't mean I got a break. During those times I was thrown in the bathroom with all of the chemicals. I was so completely helpless. All of my strength was completely gone. The punching continued. The kicking continued. The chemicals continued. The beating with anything continued. I was choked repeatedly. I didn't even have the strength to put a towel on me while I was in the bathroom. I didn't have the strength to open my eyes to even look at them anymore. I just laid there lifeless and let them have their way. After hours they were finally finished and I couldn't even make it to my bedroom. I laid there naked in the hallway unable to move.

As graduation got closer, I couldn't help but be excited that I would be away from them. But this was definitely a double-edged sword because they knew this as well so the beatings greatly increased in frequency and intensity. I never really slept that much before but now it was almost nonexistent. They would come into my room during all hours to beat me. As soon as I would walk through the door I would be beat. If they weren't home by the time I got there they would leave me notes of things to do. All the items had to be completed before they got home or I would be beat worse. The lists were always impossible to complete. I was set up to fail with each list. I eventually stopped trying so hard to complete each item on the list. I took those few hours I had by myself to rest. I had to rest at some point and time afterall. I figured as long as I got some of the more noticeable things done on the list then I could rest. I was going to get beat regardless so I had to do something for myself.

UNIVERSITY

I HAD ABSOLUTELY no desire to go to the university they chose for me to attend. I didn't care that they went there and I hated it more that it was a Christian university. At this point and time in my life, I could care less about God. He hadn't done anything for me. I prayed for years to be rid of this family or to have a new family or for them to stop or for me to die. He hadn't done any of those things. What had He done? He had made my life a living Hell. I was so done with God. I was only adamant about being involved in everything I possibly could at church because it was a safe place. My family didn't try to harm me at church. It was a public place and the façade had to continue. I got good at acting like we had the best family and like I loved my family more than anything else. In the end, after several harsh beatings, I gave in and went to the university of their choice. I didn't have much to pack as I didn't have very much at all. I was beyond ready to leave. There wasn't an ounce of sadness in me. The time came to finally say goodbye and man I couldn't be happier. I made sure the goodbye was said in a public place so they couldn't try to do anything. That night I remember laying on my bed and crying. But they weren't tears of sadness by any means. They were tears of relief. It was the first time I could breathe. It was the first time I could relax. It was the first time I could lay on my bed for an extended period of time. It was the first time I could sleep through the night and boy did I sleep. I laid in bed the majority of the next day. I didn't have any desire to get up. For once I didn't have to. For once, I didn't have to answer to anyone. Oh it was glorious! I didn't have any lists waiting for me. I didn't have my parents walking through my bedroom door. I wasn't being yelled at. I wasn't being beat. Oh and I wouldn't have to see that nail for several months! I was so excited to not see them. For once in my life I was getting what I wanted. I remember just an overall feeling of relief that overshadowed every other feeling.

When I had to start going to classes and being around people other than my roommate, things proved to be more difficult than I thought they would be. I was so completely broken as a person that I didn't have any self-esteem. I had fully believed what my parents said about me for the past 18 years. While I was on my own and finally not being beat all the time, that was the life I had grown accustomed to. This change in my life was drastic. It was hard. It was confusing. I didn't have any confidence in myself and as good as you would think things were, I found myself becoming more and more angry. My new life was incredibly difficult for me. Quite frankly I didn't know how to function without the daily dysfunction I was so used to. And since I was at a Christian University, God was shoved at me all day long and I just hated God as much as I hated my family. This only made me more angry.

To make matters worse, I would see the friends I had get letters and care packages from their families. They would talk to their families. They would talk with them while smiling and laughing. Oh this made me so mad and jealous. I would constantly get questions about my family and I would just say they were great but always busy. I hated watching my friends get mail. I felt so alone in a way that I didn't think I could. I thought I had mastered the feeling of being alone, but this was so different. My parents weren't choosing to love my friends over me, but that is how it felt. It felt like everyone around me had amazing families who loved them. Jealousy definitely played a part in my ever increasing anger. I hated that I wasn't loved and my friends all took notice of the nothing I got when they continued to get care packages. There were times when they tried to share their packages with me, but I didn't want to take away from them. And to be honest I was too angry to accept their pity.

I would frequently think back on the few good times I remembered, hoping and praying for a miracle. As full as my heart was of anger and jealousy, it was that full of hope as well. Hope that they will change. Hope that they will see me. Hope that they will love me. Hope that I will mean something good in their lives. I didn't understand my family. I didn't understand why they hated me so much. All I wanted was for their love but I would settle for them generally liking me. Looking back at the good times would fill me with temporary relief but then would pretty instantaneously fill me with extreme rage. It's a rage that is so hard to explain. It was like the Tasmanian Devil went off in me and would seep out of my pores. Anyone around me would get the brunt of that anger. Oh I wouldn't physically do anything to them, but man I sure knew how to curse like I grew up on a sailor ship. Now let's remember I was attending a Christian university and I just let it fly. Anyone in my path was going to get it and some were doing nothing more than walking to class. Add that will the goodness of God constantly being shoved down my throat....well let's just say it wasn't a good mixture.

I particularly had issues with the verses that told me to honor my parents. Oh and anything on forgiveness sent me into an instant rage fest. When I say that I hated my parents, I mean I really hated them, but I loved them too. It took me years to figure out that I didn't truly love them, I just loved the idea of a loving family. I loved the idea of a mom who loved me. Of a mom who would stand up for me. I loved the idea of a dad. The dad who protected me at all costs. I loved the idea of a big brother. The brother who wouldn't let anyone hurt me including himself. The idea of a loving family is what I loved much more than the family I was dealt. I had so many issues with this university I attended. There is nothing wrong with the university in itself. It has to do with the fact that it was where my parents went to school. It was where my grandfather wanted me to go to school. It was where my parents met and fell in love. I couldn't help but see them throughout the campus and that was the last thing I wanted to see. I wanted to be on my own. I wanted to be rid of them in every way possible. I wanted to be rid of God. Being forced to be where I had no desire to be only added fuel to the rage fire inside of me.

SCHOOL BREAKS

SCHOOL BREAKS WERE always a problem. What was I supposed to do? I had nowhere to go but back home. And oh my family ate this up. They knew I wouldn't have anywhere else to go. They knew I was worthless and that nobody could love me or like me. And I played right into their hands. I had no other choice. Now It was a four hour drive back to Neosho, if I went the speed limit. Now we all know that I didn't and that four hour drive would be extended by several hours but the end result was always the same. The last hour of the drive would be filled with extreme anxiety. The kind where you can't breathe and your whole body shakes. The kind that makes you pull over and stop several times before you can push forward. Tears would stream down my face that entire last hour. My driving was like a lost grandma out on her Sunday afternoon drive. I knew what was waiting for me at home and that fear about did me in with each trip back. They had saved up the beating for so long that I couldn't even get out of my car before they were on top of me. I couldn't even get my bag out until sometime the next day, if I had the courage to go out of the house to get it. The beatings were fierce and would last the entire trip. They were unrelenting in every sort of way. By the time breaks rolled around my body had gotten used to getting more sleep (although let's be honest, it wasn't ever that much). My body had gotten used to not having to listen for every little sound. My body had gotten used to not being in a constant state of fight-flight-freeze, but now with every trip back home, that came to a screeching halt. It was absolutely horrible.

As I pulled into the driveway and rounded the curve, I could see them standing there waiting for me. It was a feeling of pure dread and fear. They would always say, "There she is. It's so good to see you." In such sinister voices. The kind of voices where you know things are about to get really bad. I was usually yanked out of the car and thrown around outside. The punches would come in flying and I would always get in trouble for not being home sooner. Being thrown against the car had so many advantages to them because your head goes back and immediately exposes your throat. It was the perfect choke hold opportunity for them. I believe they would dream about my school breaks and think about what they would do much like you would count down for a vacation and make your plans for while you are there. *Oh fuck, quit choking me!!! Let go! Quit punching me and throwing me wherever you damn well please! God Damnit!!!! Shit, shit, shit, shit.* Here they go with another round. Outside beatings were a whole different ball game because our driveway was gravel and not just the pea size gravel. The gravel we are talking about ranged from pea size to softball size. The rocks would be thrown down on me like hail zipping to the ground. There was no ducking and covering. When your perpetrators are only a few feet away and throwing any size of rocks at you as hard as they possibly can, it hurts beyond belief. It cuts deep into your skin and bruises instantaneously. All I could think about was how much I wished I could just get back in the car and never come back here again. I knew it wasn't possible though and I knew I would eventually die at their hands.

When they were done with me outside, I would be drug by my hair up the steps and into the house. The kicking would ensue with brutal force. My body was already ragged and worn from everything that had just happened outside. *Please just stop! Why can't you just love me? Why can't you be happy to see me for once? Why can't I ever be enough for you? Why do you have to do this? What did I do this time? Just stop and love me!* The kicking was coming from both sides all at once. It was so hard to breathe due to the force of the blows. I had learned many years ago to just be there and take it. If I showed any sort of emotion, I only got it worse. I had to go into this place deep inside of me to distance myself from the pain I was having to endure. I had to go into my shell and build my walls up.

I had to make it to where they couldn't penetrate the tears brimming on my eyes with each and every blow. Before I knew it my body was getting drug over that damn nail. I never knew I could hate an inanimate object so much. Once I was bleeding profusely they stood me up and my mother slapped me as hard as she could across my face. She then emphasized each word with a hard slap, "You are an ungrateful piece of shit. You are nothing bitch. You are the worst possible thing that could have ever happened to this family." Before I could even recover from the slapping, the punching started back up. Immediately the breath was knocked out of me as the first, second, third, fourth, and fifth punch was to my stomach. Then another round of slaps, then right back to the punching. It was rapid fire and there was no way to keep up. I just knew I had to keep my composure. I had to stay locked away in my shell. I could scream and cry all I wanted in my head but I couldn't dare let any of that slip out. I was then back down on the ground with my father's hands pushing down on my neck. Each time he did this, I knew for sure it was going to be the last thing I saw and felt before I died. The pressure was different than when he had his hands wrapped around my neck and I was pushed against something. In this position his full body weight was forcefully being pushed through his arms and down to his hands and onto my neck. There was no swallowing or breathing. Not even a little bit. The panic I felt immediately sent me into a panic attack. The fear I felt was so sudden, I didn't even know what to do with it. The rage I saw in his eyes was that of a madman. With each passing second the pain became less as the panic took over. The panic of knowing I was completely helpless. The panic of knowing he was so angry with me that he was finding joy in killing me. The panic of knowing this was how my life was going to end. Just as the panic had completely enveloped me and my eyes couldn't stay open any longer, he let go, but before I could even take in a breath he punched me repeatedly. He then picked me up and threw me across the room. He didn't care where I landed or what table got broken. All he cared about was hurting me. The last place I landed was right by a lamp. He grabbed the cord and yanked it out of the wall and began to beat me with it. He didn't care where he was hitting me, just as long as he could see the stripes he was making. His belt soon came flying off and my mother grabbed the yard stick she kept by her chair. There were several times during this beating where I was made to stand up and bend over furniture. There were also several times during this beating where I was made to stand up, hold my arms up or out and take the beating. They never tired of seeing the marks they were making on me. Of seeing the blood pouring out. Of seeing the bruises and broken bones. I wondered how much more my body could take. *Keep going Suzanne. They aren't going to stop, but if you stop being strong, it will only get worse. I can't imagine worse. What else would they do? Don't think about the pain. Think of something else.....anything else.* The swings were coming at rapid speed. You could hear that awful swish through the air right before you heard the snap on bare skin. *God I hate coming home. I need to find some excuse to not come back.* Every inch of me was covered in welts. I was a deep shade of red from the top of my neck to the bottom of my feet. Once they finished they looked at me and said, "It's so good for you to be home." I knew what they were saying and I knew they were happy for me to be home because then their scapegoat was back. Their punching bag was back. The feeling of satisfaction they gained from hurting me was back. They weren't happy I was back because they loved me. No that was far from it. They were just happy I was back so they could have their way with me.

My remaining time at home was much the same. It was constant lists that were impossible to complete followed by horrendous beatings. The little weight I had gained while at school quickly came off as I was no longer allowed to eat and was forced to throw up. Being at home was a nightmare. *How much longer till I can go back to school? How much longer do I have to endure this? I just want to be loved. I want my parents to love me. I want to be like everyone else. Why can't I make them happy? Why do they hate me so much? I'm truly no good for anything. I won't ever do anything right. No one will ever love me. There is no way I am going to ever get out from under them. I am so completely worthless.* The rage fueled inside of me and just festered since I couldn't let it out in any way. I had no time to myself. I had no hope whatsoever.

COURAGE

I LASTED A year and a half at the university of their choice before I found some crazy courage. I absolutely hated where I was and with each trip back home I would stop at the University of Arkansas in Fayetteville and spend some time with friends. Sometimes it would just be a few hours and other times it would be for several days. During these trips I had made several other friends. I didn't know it at the time, but I had met the person that would save me.

Slowly but also quickly, I began to open up to her. I didn't by any means tell her everything but I did tell her enough. And she believed me. It was amazing! I had thought for years that maybe I truly was lying about it all. That maybe it was just a horrible dream. But then I would look down at my body and know that there was no way it was all made up. Somebody had to believe me and finally somebody did. She began to encourage me to get away from them. To cut ties with them, but that is so much easier said than done. I was still attending their university but I knew I needed to be with these new friends. I wanted to go to school where I wanted to go, not where they were making me go. After a lot of convincing and late night phone calls and text messages (now this was when each text message was 10 cents....needless to say we racked up a HUGE phone bill) I took the plunge. That school break I was going to tell them that I was no longer going to go where they wanted me to go. I was going to go to the University of Arkansas. My new but very close friend decided she would go to Neosho with me to tell them because I was so afraid. I knew it had to be done. I knew I needed to tell them. And this was the first time I was really taking charge of my life. I wasn't going to be ruled by them anymore.

When we arrived at the house, they were quite shocked. I hadn't told them I was bringing anyone with me. They were waiting outside like they normally were, but they didn't get the chance to do anything since I had brought along a friend. *Hahahahaha I outsmarted you! I have someone with me who cares about me. I have someone here that will protect me from you monsters. Hahahaha you can't touch me. Now you have to put on your façade behind your closed doors.* Oh how I felt good. The anxiety completely washed away. I had them and they couldn't do anything about it. For once they were the helpless ones. Oh my how the tables had turned. I couldn't help but smile from ear to ear. I felt so free and on top of the world. I had finally done something right regardless of how reckless it was. There was this weight lifted off of my shoulders when I knew they had to play into their façade they had created. Oh how there was rage in their eyes. There was more rage there than there was when I was almost killed so many times. More rage then when they brought the knife on me. Oh but I knew they had to keep that rage inside of them and I felt happy. It was the first time I felt truly happy in that house. And it was all because, I talked, and my friend believed me.

Now over the past couple of months nothing happened as long as my brother was there. I don't know why there was this change in him. Maybe it was his time in jail. Maybe it was him constantly failing out of college. Maybe it was something in him changing, but he didn't allow them to beat me in his presence. I honestly didn't care what it was, I was just thankful for it. So the next day when he was at the house, I knew I was now doubly protected. I was elated. Now don't get me wrong, I didn't like the guy. I despised the guy, but I was glad when he walked through the door.

The lists didn't stop just because I had a friend there. However, the beatings did. But instead of me doing everything by myself, she pitched in to help. And I was oh so thankful. The lists never got completed but they seemed more manageable with another person helping. In between doing chores, we had decided to sit down and talk to them about me leaving their university and transferring to the University of Arkansas. I was nervous to talk to them about this even with my brother there and my friend. I didn't know if they would stop the façade or if they cared too much about their reputation to keep it going. I had no idea how to start the conversation and my voice was quite shaky. When I told them I was leaving at the end of the semester, they were silent. Now I knew this to be the festering kind of anger and it was almost scarier than them screaming and shouting. I stayed silent and waited for what seemed like an eternity for them to talk. "No." said my father. "You will not be transferring." Now this is where that crazy courage came into play because I said, with a much stronger voice, "I will be transferring. I will not be going to Harding anymore after this semester. I will be starting at the University of Arkansas next semester." "No, you won't." said my mother. This turned into a "No you won't", "Yes I will" argument. Finally my father asked, "Why?" My answer was simple. It wasn't rehearsed in any sort of way, just simple. "I don't want to go where you tell me to go. I have never wanted to go to Harding and have always wanted to go to the University of Arkansas. I don't care about going to a Christian university. I am an adult and I am able to make my own decisions as to where I will be attending school." This is when my father popped out of his chair and marched over to me. His finger pointing and wagging the whole way. "You will NOT be changing schools! You will NOT go to the University of Arkansas! You WILL stay at Harding! You do NOT get to make decisions! You ARE a little baby girl who isn't smart enough to do anything! You will NOT talk back to us again! You WILL stay at Harding and there will not be another word about this!" And with that last statement he slapped me hard across my face with my friend sitting right there. I was dumbfounded. They hadn't ever crossed this line in front of people. This was new. But I am telling you, I had stupid, crazy courage. Anybody who had grown up like I had, would have the brains to shut up and not say anything else, but I had the stupid courage. I turned my head and looked my father right in his eyes with a deep determination and said in an unwavering voice, "I will not be going back to Harding at the end of the semester. I will be transferring to the University of Arkansas, the school of my choosing." This time, it was my mother who popped out of her chair. I don't think my friend knew what to do. I think she was caught in between shock, dismay, and confusion, but just having her beside me was enough to give me the courage. "Did you not hear your father you little bitch? "This is not up for discussion! You do NOT talk back to us! You DO as we say! You don't have another option. You will remain at Harding! I don't care what you want bitch!" And with that came another couple of hard slaps. Once again the stupid courage took over. I set my face square and looked in her eyes with the same determination and said, "I will not be going back to Harding at the end of the semester. I will be transferring to the University of Arkansas, the school of my choosing." At this point they were flabbergasted. There was rage in their eyes mixed with doubt, confusion, questioning, and shock. My voice had become stronger than anything they had ever heard despite their slaps in front of my friend. The slaps only made me more determined. The yelling only made my voice stronger. My words didn't need to change, just my tonality and inflection. For the first time, I got up, walked around them and left the room. My body was tense as I was turning my back on them, but I remained strong. I walked with my shoulders held high and my chin up.

I walked to my room and shut the door. The instant it was shut I slumped to the floor. I was exhausted, relieved, proud, but also terrified. That stupid courage wears a person out. I stayed on the floor even though I was terrified, I also had a smile on my face. A smile that only came from a sense of being proud. It was a feeling I hadn't felt before. Sure I had been proud of myself during various sporting events, but this was a whole different kind of proud. The proud that comes from facing your fears head on.

STUPID COURAGE PART 2

AFTER A WHILE it was determined that my friend and I needed to switch out laundry (as we only washed our own and none of theirs). I told my friend to go ahead and go downstairs to switch the laundry and I would go in the living room and get our coats out of the closet. She was very hesitant to leave me alone after witnessing the slaps, but I told her it was ok. My brother was in the living room, so I didn't believe anything would happen. Oh how wrong I could be! There was pushing and punching and throwing the second she got down the stairs. Of course she had no way of knowing this. I told them I was just getting our coats and then would be going back to the bedroom. My father said to me, "You will not be going anywhere except 6 feet under." I prayed for my friend to get back upstairs. To completely forget about the laundry and just telepathically know that I needed her. I was shoved into the wall with such force the wind was knocked out of me. But I couldn't gasp for air because my father's hands were around my neck squeezing as hard as they possibly could. His thumbs were pushing farther and farther in until I thought he was going to break my neck. He lifted me off of the ground and was holding me against the wall by my neck. I could see a difference in his eyes. This was a different kind of rage. I had completely dismissed him earlier and disrespected him. All of those other times I was for sure I was going to die didn't compare to this. I remember kicking trying to get him off of me but it only made him squeeze tighter and tighter. I don't remember anything after that.

When I came to, I was in the car and my friend was driving. She later told me, she walked up the stairs and saw what was happening. She doesn't have a "freeze" like I do, she went full force "fight" and got me out of there. She told me she picked me up over her shoulders and immediately took me to the car. She said my parents were screaming and shouting that they didn't do anything wrong. That I had asked my father to kill me while she was gone. That I had asked for it. We didn't stop at a hospital. We didn't stop anywhere. She woke me up when we got to her house.

That was the last time I have ever stepped foot in my parents' house. And I will never go back. I have no good memories of that house except for the time I had stupid courage, but even that didn't last long. It ended with me almost dead. If my friend wasn't there, I would not have made it out alive. I truly would be six feet under. I thank God for that friend having an open heart and ears to hear my story. To be there for that conversation and ultimately for saving my life.

BACK TO SCHOOL

AFTER I RECOVERED and was able to swallow and use my voice again, my time away from school had come to a close. The bruises were still present on my neck but I couldn't miss any more school. I went back to Harding and knew I would be leaving and with that departure I was beginning the process of being free of my family. I knew it was going to be a fight leaving, but I had more determination now than ever before. As the semester came to a close I was ready to go. Once in Fayetteville, I ended up staying with my friend and her two roommates until she and I could find an apartment. I didn't have any money because my parents would take all of my money out of my bank and routinely leave me in the negative. My friends parents did not care for me because they didn't think I would be a good influence on their daughter. They didn't know me and assumed I would just be using her for money. I tried to reassure them that wasn't the case, but here I was moving in with their daughter with no way to pay for anything. My plan was to start school at the University of Arkansas in the Spring semester; however, that plan fell through. Harding would not release my transcript without me giving them $10, 000. You see, not only did I not have any money, I had also been flagged by student loan companies. In order to get student loans then, you had to have your parents income and tax information. I absolutely hated this because it meant I had to rely on them for something else. I didn't know, but they gave me incorrect information and I agreed that the information was correct when I submitted the paperwork. Long story short, I didn't get the loans because of this. I also couldn't get student loans for several more years after this. But before I could even do anything at the University of Arkansas, they had to have my transcript from Harding. I was at my parents mercy once again. I called them and asked them why they had done this. I was simply told, I was the one who lied, not them. I am the one who gets myself into these messes and now I would have to be stuck at Harding. They laughed about the whole situation and said, "See, you don't amount to anything. You can't even fill out paperwork correctly." I ended up getting a private loan to pay the $10,000, but I still had the problem of paying for the University of Arkansas. I called everyone I knew to see if they would co-sign on a loan with me, but I was always too late. My parents had gotten to them first and told them I was telling lies and just looking for some attention. Every person ended up saying no. It was completely hopeless. The determination I once felt was gone. I wasn't going to go back to Harding. But what was I supposed to do about school?

There wasn't anything else for me to do except search for a job. A full-time job. Something that could at least pay the bills so my friends parents didn't think I was completely worthless. After two months of searching, I landed on a job at a day care. The director went to the church I was attending with my friend and she seemed to employ several college students from the church. It wasn't the best pay in the world, but it was enough to pay the bills, well it should have been enough. It would have been enough if my parents hadn't kept stealing money from me. When I finally had enough cash to pull myself out of the negative and to start my own account that is exactly what I did. I shut down the other one and put one in just my name. I also made sure in this account it stated who had access to it and who didn't. Now, when two money hungry people suddenly don't have access to the funds they were stealing, they become outraged. That was a horrible phone call. You see at this point; I was still holding onto the hope that they would change. If I defied them and they stopped getting what they wanted, I truly believed they would change. I also really struggled with the fact that they were my parents. They were my family. No matter how awful they were, I still loved them to some degree. I was sad and heartbroken when my friend would talk to her parents. Or when her parents would visit. All I wanted was to have parents like that. I just wanted my parents to love me. Seeing other people have that relationship with their family was like knives stabbing my heart. But that hope was still there regardless of how many times they let me down. So I was still answering their phone calls hoping to no end that this would be the time they would cry and apologize. This would be the time they said the loved me. This would be the time; I could be their daughter again. This was the time that they had changed. But with each phone call, I was sadly mistaken. They demanded to know my account information. They demanded for me to put my money into the other account. They demanded for me to give them my money because that is my duty as their daughter. They demanded to know where I was living so they could come get the money themselves. And with each heartbreaking phone call, my determination was slowly growing. They were not going to receive any of that information from me and I didn't have this duty as their daughter. I said as little as I could during those phone calls, but I clearly said "No" to each demand.

For almost four months I couldn't help with the bills. My friends parents were thinking the worse of me and I didn't know it at the time but would routinely talk to my friend about kicking me out. All they saw in me was somebody they didn't want their daughter to associate with. They saw a mooch. They saw an angry individual who obviously had no plan. They just didn't know that my plan shattered into pieces and it was impossible to

EXTRACTING SUZANNE

recover any of it.

When I started working at the day care, it became quite apparent that I didn't really know what I was doing. Oh I had babysat a lot when I was younger to get a little bit of money. I had changed diapers. I had fed the kids and played with them, but when it came to really taking care of the kids, I didn't know what I was doing. It was a big learning curve for sure. I was eager to learn and was mentored by a wonderful teacher. I slowly began to gain a little bit of confidence and was soon blossoming at the day care. I then became the afternoon shift manager. I felt proud of myself for learning what was needed and for proving myself trustworthy especially when I was told so many times that I was just a liar.

Slowly I began to change how my friends parents viewed me. At one point I had even tried to start paying them back, but they wouldn't accept it. Because of my job and the added responsibilities in my job I was able to consistently pay my share of the bills. I began going with my friend to her parents' house (it was only 45 minutes away) and getting to know them. I was highly skeptical. Afterall there was only one adult in my life that had ever believed anything I had said. While I was skeptical, I was also very timid. I didn't want to say much or really be around them for fear of doing the wrong thing. When they would have normal family arguments, I would become frightened and stay in the room. I wasn't able to come out. I couldn't bear getting beat by someone else. I couldn't force myself to move. I was frozen in the bedroom. It was my hiding place. It was the place where I felt the safest even though they could come into the room at any point and time. With time, I became a little more comfortable around them, but I knew there were constant arguments between my friend and her parents about me. I didn't want to open up to them. I honestly had no desire. My friend and I would get into constant arguments about telling her parents. She would tell me that her family isn't like my family. She would tell me that they would believe me and want to help. She made valid points; I just didn't believe a word she said. My past had told me otherwise. My past had told me that if I told people, I would be beat till I wished I was dead, but I eventually gave in. I didn't see any way around it and if I wanted to stay with my friend, then I had to do something. I felt like I had no choice.

We drove to her parents' house and all sat down in the living room. After several moments of awkward silence, I finally began to talk with the help of my friend. I didn't get much out before her father popped out of his chair and came walking towards me and then at the last second turned and walked out of the room. I immediately fell silent and frozen in place. I knew for sure he was coming over to beat me like my parents had done on so many occasions. I couldn't speak. I couldn't move. I could barely take in shallow breaths. I was transported to my parents living room instead of my friends living room. I didn't see them. I saw the wall where I was choked. I saw the nail that dug into me. I saw the floral chair in the corner. I saw the entertainment center. I saw the coffee table. I saw the oversized chair. And I saw my parents. I saw the rage in their eyes and felt the hard slaps across my face. I felt my body being lifted off of the couch and thrown into the wall. I felt the kicking and punching. I heard the screaming and name calling. I heard their evil cackles as I writhed in pain. As I sat there, words wouldn't form anymore. My head hung as I was put into submission. Eventually when I came back and realized it was my friends living room, she was talking and her father was back. I was still sitting in the same position with my fists clenched tight. My friend did the rest of the talking and when it was over, I went to bed. I was exhausted. I didn't sleep that night. Every sound woke me up. I was hypervigilant just like I was when I was living in Neosho. I couldn't lay still. I would toss and turn on the bed. When I got tired of the bed I moved to the floor. No matter where I was, I couldn't sleep. I was filled with fear. I just knew my parents were going to find out and I would surely die this time. I was so certain that my friends parents were going to turn out just like mine. They were obviously upset and I knew it was directed at me. It was antagonizing waiting for the impeding beating to happen.

I wished they would just hurry up and get the beating over with. I was tired of waiting so I eventually went out of the bedroom. I sat down in the living room. The way they looked at me was different than it was before. Their eyes were different as well as how they held themselves. There was a change in them and this made me even more apprehensive, but I stayed out in the living room. Throughout the course of the day, they did not beat me. I had learned long ago that if the beating didn't happen right away, it would happen eventually. I was on pins and needles the whole day, but the beating never came. The beating didn't happen the next day or the day after that either. My anxiety was incredibly high just waiting for hell to break loose. While I was waiting for hell to break loose, I was watching their every move. Watching their eyes, studying their body language, hearing the different tonalities as they talked so I could be one step ahead of them. So I could tell when the beating was going to take place. Studying them so closely was the only thing that kept the panic at bay. It gave me something to do.

They then asked to talk to me and that panic of mine went through the roof. I sat down in the same spot in the living room. The proceeded to tell me that they would help me in any way they possibly could. They were very sorry for what had happened to me. They took me in and gave me hugs and her dad apologized for the way he reacted when I was trying to tell them. A part of me relaxed a little while the other part of me told me relaxing wasn't an option. I was in a complete state of confusion. This wasn't anything I could have predicted. I was relieved that they believed me but I had absolutely no trust that they would truly be there for me. They told me I was part of their family now and they would help me get away from my family. They told me I would be their adopted daughter. Now I was 18 at the time, so no paperwork for official adoption took place. For someone to want me as a daughter was more than what I could possibly imagine. For the first time in my life, someone truly wanted me. Someone truly cared about me. I believe on that day, when they were told, their ideas about me changed completely. They didn't see me as a mooch anymore. They didn't see me as someone whom they didn't want their daughter to associate with. They simply saw me as a very broken individual. I didn't want their pity, but honestly pity was a nice change from beatings.

SCHOOL?

OH FINANCES! WHAT was I going to do about school? I now had a steady job and was paying my fair share of everything as well as being able to purchase a few extras here and there. Things were starting to look up. I was still very much an angry individual, but I could at least pay for things. I knew I HAD to get back to school, but I just didn't know how. I would spend hours thinking about what to do, of who I could ask to help. I would make lists of potential people but they would end up getting marked off as my parents had already gotten to them. It was hopeless. I had finally decided what I wanted to major in but didn't know if I would be able to anymore. After writing another list once again, I took a chance on some people who went to my parents church, but they didn't know them really well. I didn't really know them. I really only knew of them. So I set up a meeting with them and asked them if they would co-sign the loan. I promised them I would never default on it. I promised them I would pay it back as fast as I could. I showed them the plan and all of the paperwork. I even had a representative on the phone to answer any additional questions. I went into this like a business meeting. The only thing I didn't have was a PowerPoint presentation. I explained to them that my parents weren't able to help pay for college due to unfortunate events. I wasn't about to go into detail about what the unfortunate events were. I just knew this was my last chance to get back to school. It was my chance to prove my parents wrong. It was a chance to be openly defiant and take charge of my life. It was a chance to shock them once again. And shock them I did when the loan had all of the necessary signatures on it. It was official. I would be an Arkansas Razorback in the fall. Everything was in order. I had taken charge of my life and I was moving one step closer to getting out from under my family.

Oh man they were mad, but they couldn't find me. Now that doesn't mean that they didn't try because they did. They would frequently go down to Fayetteville in hopes of getting their hands on me, but I knew the town. I knew the backroads and the side streets. I knew how to maneuver away from them. There was one store in which I came within five feet of them. I dropped everything I had and got out of there. They followed me but I was able to lose them in traffic. Years later I found out they would come to Fayetteville for the high school sporting events hoping I was there. I was terrified of my family. I knew if they got their hands on me, I would never see the light of day again. I would never see anyone because I was dead. I had absolutely no doubt they would kill me if they could just get me in their grasps again. My life had turned into a deadly game of cat and mouse. I was always on the lookout for their vehicle or anybody that looked like them. When I saw vehicles that were the same as theirs I would freeze in fear. They were always on the search for me and I was always watching my back.

HOPE BEYOND HOPE

MY FRIEND AND I had some extremely difficult times to say the least. Growing up I wasn't allowed to show any emotion. Her upbringing was much different. They yelled, talked and then moved on all in a span of a couple of minutes. I would just concede to whatever she wanted all the time. She wanted to have discussions. I didn't know how. I had no idea that you could even have discussions without getting hit. I would keep everything bottled up inside, just the way I was taught. As I became more comfortable with her, I realized she wouldn't beat me. She kept pushing me to change. Telling me what was wrong with me and what I needed to do about it. I didn't necessarily feel like I should be the only person who had to change in order to make a friendship work. I had finally had enough and I completely exploded. I was screaming and yelling at her.

I was slamming doors and punching the pillows. I would quit talking to her all together. I would lock myself away. I would curse and say hurtful words. I didn't know what had come over me. I didn't know how to control it. It was like the years of rage bottled up inside of me came erupting out during each argument. I didn't care if what I said hurt her. I didn't care if she agreed or not, I was just going to scream it at the top of my lungs. The rage monster came out with a vengeance. The rage monster continued to come erupting out until one day she looked at me and said, "I don't see Suzanne in those eyes. All I see is your father. The father who hurt you in every sort of way is who you are turning into."

Oh man, beat me instead. Lock me in a chemical bathroom. Choke me. Break my bones. Drag me over the nail. Lock me outside. Have someone rape me. Starve me. Tell me I'm a mistake. Do anything in the world except tell me that I am becoming my father and that is all you see in my eyes. That remark cut me deeper than anything my family had ever done to me. I didn't talk to my friend for several days after that. I completely ignored her. I stayed as far away as possible. I couldn't believe she had said that to me. I didn't know how to express any sort of emotion. I needed Emotions for Dummies. I needed a class on what to call the various emotions and what you were supposed to do with them. It was becoming clear that I was stuck. That I had nowhere to turn. I really should have picked up on this sign but I was so starved for someone to love me, that I let it be. I decided right then and there, I would have to crawl back into my shell.

My friend started pushing me to go to a therapist. She didn't know about the previous times and I didn't really feel like telling her. I would tell her I would think about it and then never did. There were weekly one-sided arguments over this issue. Each time she brought it up, I felt like such a failure. I felt like everything my family said about me was true. I felt like everyone would look down on me for going to therapy. I felt isolated and like I was the cause of all of the problems. I knew my friend was stubborn enough that she would keep bringing it up. But I wasn't brave enough to express my anxieties. Afterall, trying to express myself (yes, I was a rage monster, but at the time I only saw it as trying to get things off of my chest) made her say some awful things about me. I wasn't about to go down that road again. The more she brought it up, the more awful I felt about myself. The more depressed I became. The angrier I became. The more I grew into my shell.

There was a therapist at the church we were attending. I was told I would be able to see her for free for a certain amount of sessions. Going to therapy was the last thing I needed. It hadn't done any good before. In fact it created a whole big mess, but I was also so extremely tired of the constant nagging. So the appointment was set up. I drove myself to the church. And that's all that happened. I never made it to that appointment. I never even got out of my car. I sat there feeling completely heartbroken. Full of anxiety. Full of fear. Full of hopelessness. I felt truly worthless. I felt exactly how my parents wanted me to feel. They were right about everything.

When I got back home my friend immediately asked me how the session went. I told her I went but never made it inside. That I ended up just sitting in my car. This did not make her happy. She wanted me to go to therapy more than anything. She kept saying it was good for me and I needed to do it. She said it didn't matter what other people thought and that I just needed to get over it. There was no "getting over it". You don't just get over what happened. I wanted to please my friend. I wanted to make her happy. But at the same time I was attempting to be more on my own. I was for the first time truly experiencing the world. There were several more arguments about therapy. And once again, I gave in. I promised myself that this time would be different. I would make it into the appointment and not break down in tears in my car. I would 'get over it' and walk into that office. It took every ounce of courage I had to turn off the ignition in my car. Then it took more courage to take off my seatbelt and open the door. Still the courage kept coming as I walked up to the church doors. Once again that courage filled me, to ask for the therapist and then to walk down the long hallway to her office. At that point I needed every ounce of that stupid courage to knock on her door, paint a smile on my face, and walk into her office.

I had made it in. Now to start the talking, but that didn't really happen past the formalities. I didn't know what to say. When she asked me why I was there, I told her it was because my friend was annoyingly persistent about it. We sat there in some very awkward silence, but the longer it went, the less awkward it became for me. I was a veteran at this silence treatment at the therapists. She then started asking questions that didn't have any relevance whatsoever. Questions like, what was my favorite season, if I like oceans or mountains better, what my favorite food was, etc. I didn't think anything of it at the time, but looking back, I can see how she was able to slowly climb herself up one of my fortress walls and take just a peak into me. We set up the next appointment and then it was over.

I told my friend that the therapist and I talked. I also told her we set up another appointment. But I didn't tell her what we talked about. When it was time for my next appointment I was filled with that same anxiety. I had to talk myself into driving to the church, to turning off the car, to getting out of the car, to taking each and every step to her office. After the greetings, we sat down to silence again. The last session wasn't bad, but I was still waiting for the ceiling to drop. I was waiting for my parents to jump out at any point and time. She then began to ask me more nonsense questions. This cycle of therapy went on for several sessions. Several more than I would like to admit, but it kept me going back.

Once I had become more comfortable with the therapist, I would answer her more serious questions with a very tip of the iceberg type of answer. Then therapy progressed from there. But while therapy was progressing, my friend and I were getting into more and more arguments. I was still so completely filled with a deep anger that seemed to seep out of me. One particular argument we had on several occasions was about me going to church. I had absolutely no desire to go to church on any sort of consistent basis. I couldn't stand God. He was the cause of all of my issues. He was the cause of all of my pain. He did all of this. At least that is what I truly believed at the time. She would even go so far as telling me she would pull me over her shoulder in my pajamas and take me into church if I didn't get out of bed and go. At this point, she would have. She has a very strong personality and if she wants something or if she believes in something, nothing and nobody will make her back down. I was lucky she believed me about my family because then I was able to live.

THE TURNING OF A FRIEND

CHARLOTTE ALSO WENT to the University of Arkansas. I don't think she was very happy when I transferred there. I think she thought I would steal all of her friends and be needy. That wasn't my intention by any means, but I also wanted my friend. She was the only positive thing in my life for so many years. I couldn't stomach losing her as well.

My parents are master manipulators. They can make you feel sorry for them in .2 seconds. I have witnessed this firsthand with various of people. They have this ability to turn people from one point of view to their point of view. When someone has the capability, little hope is found in people believing you. Charlotte would go home to visit quite often and would go to church where my father would regularly lead singing, prayers or communion.

Without me in the picture right there, my parents took full advantage of Charlotte. They ended up turning her.

We were on a retreat now that I was going to school at the University of Arkansas, I was officially a member of the Razorbacks for Christ. My parents had just called me and screamed at me while calling me every name in the book. Every ounce of self-esteem I had worked so hard to acquire, would be completely destroyed by them in a matter of seconds. I was still afraid of them. I knew if I didn't answer my phone something worse was going to happen so I always answered and stayed on the line. They would tell me how worthless I was, how big of a mistake I was. They would tell me everything that I was doing wrong. They would tell me that I owed them money and it was my duty to give them all of mine. They would threaten me and badger me. They would go round and round in circles saying the same thing just in different ways. Rationally you think, just hang up the phone, but trauma brain doesn't allow you to do that. So I sat there listening to each and every word. Soaking it all in and believing it. When I got off the phone with them I was devastated. I just looked up at the stars as tears streamed down my face. Charlotte came outside since I had been gone for a while to see what was going on. I explained everything to her in between sobs. As she was hugging me she said, "Your parents deserve to be treated better than the way you treat them. You haven't called them. You haven't gone back to Neosho to see them. Think about how you are making them feel. They deserve better." After she was finished I slowly pulled away. I looked at her and said, "I can't believe you just said that. You saw the markings and the broken body parts. You saw firsthand what happened and this is what you say to me." I turned my back on her and continued to look up at the stars as tears fell from my eyes. I expected to be hurt by them, but I never expected her to hurt me. I never saw this coming. The one person who I was the most vulnerable with, turned on me. The person who cleaned up the blood and reapplied bandages. The person who was my best friend. The person I promised I wouldn't go anywhere near suicide again because I didn't want to hurt her, has shattered me. From that point on, our relationship was split like a giant fissure. Nothing could ever make that friendship go back to what it used to be and from that point on, I never trusted anything she said. Each and every time she went back to Neosho I was suspicious. I was always waiting for her to say something and many times she did. I truly believe she thought she was doing the right thing and for that I can't blame her. I know how my parents use people and make it seem like the best and the most right thing to do. I can't blame her for falling into their trap, but that never takes the pain away. I was excited to be around my best friend again when I moved to Fayetteville, but now I only dreaded her presence. I wanted our friendship to go back to what it was. My happiest moments were with her despite all of the abuse. But I knew our friendship would only become less and less as my hurt grew.

RAZORBACKS FOR CHRIST

AT THE UNIVERSITY of Arkansas there was this amazing group called the Razorbacks For Christ (RFC). My friend was already part of this group and I slowly became more involved with them. When I started school, that involvement drastically increased. We would always be gathering together for something. For the first time, I felt like I belonged somewhere. It wasn't an instant feeling of belonging but one that gradually grew as I became more involved. It was a feeling unlike anything I had ever had. In high school when I was playing sports or in band, I knew my role was important. I felt like I belonged, but not in the way I was feeling now. I felt like I was truly part of something and the people there truly cared for one another. I had a family with the RFCs. It was the first time I had ever experienced something like that. We would genuinely enjoy the company of each other.

We would gather for Tuesday night devos and the songs would engulf the area. My view on God was slowly changing. While we were singing (it was all acapella) I could feel God. I could hear God. I love all kinds of music, but there is something special about hearing four-part harmony during praise and worship. While singing the words would resonate with me. It was as if the songs were picked out just for me. I lived for those Tuesday night devos.

The RFCs were a hoot of a bunch! We were always doing something. It might have been the beginning of the year Olympics or a scavenger hunt. Maybe it was watching movies, going bowling and getting ice cream. Maybe it was playing volleyball until you couldn't see the ball anymore. Or hiking and camping and playing ultimate frisbee. Maybe it was walking around looking at all of the Christmas lights and ice skating. It was going on road trips to see friends. It was mission trips and VBS. It was studying for all hours in a coffee shop. It was late night Denny's so we could take a break from schoolwork. It was playing in the snow and being there for each other during ice storms. It was going on ski trips and playing games. It was jumping in the creek and getting the worse sunburn ever. It was helping each other move oh so many times. It was laughing and loving. It was being with one another and it was the best time of my life. The RFCs were my family. They made me smile. They made me laugh. They made me feel comfortable. None of these things I had ever experienced before.

As great as it was to be feeling these things, they also came with fear, anxiety, and panic. I was so terrified that if they knew the real story of me, they would turn just like Charlotte did. I was afraid I was going to lose it all. I was struck with panic each and every time Charlotte came back from Neosho. I didn't want anyone to find out about my family. I was waiting for the day my parents would show up at an RFC event. I was so ashamed. The abuse was my fault. I was only getting what I deserved and if I had just obeyed, then I wouldn't have to be punished. This fear continued to grow stronger with the closer I grew to the RFCs. As much as I loved being with them, I had to talk myself into each and every activity. It was exhausting!

CONTINUED THERAPY

I CONTINUED TO go to my therapy sessions and didn't miss anymore unless I was sick. Oh the panic attacks leading up to them never stopped but my feet continued to take steps into her office. The therapy was changing and we were diving a little deeper with each session. I was beginning to open up to her more. As we dove deeper, my anger intensified. I was so resentful of my family. I became more and more jealous of my friend and her relationship with her family. I became infuriated when I saw parents taking care of their children. My fury waged on deeper and deeper. I absolutely hated my family with every fiber of my being. It was such a deep hatred that burned throughout my body. I didn't even know you could be so angry all the time. I thought of all of the ways to hurt them. I dreamed of the ways they would die in pain and suffering. I came up with elaborate plans on what I would do if I saw them again. I fed my hatred all day long. I would write about all the wrongs they did. I believed I had every right to hurt them. I would write for hours about how I would get my revenge and oh it made me feel good. It made me feel powerful. It fed my soul in a way that nothing else had. It was such a wonderful feeling. I dreamed of their cries and what it would sound like. I dreamed about laughing in their pain. I dreamed of their screams and all of the hurtful things I would say to them. I dreamed about what their faces would look like while I was punching them, while I had that knife pushing into them, while I broke their bones. I dreamed of this turn of events. This deep hatred fueled me, but it also came at a cost. While I was feeling powerful, the rage took over my life. It didn't take much for me to snap. It could be something as simple as someone walking beside me and I didn't want them there. It could be that a class was canceled and it was inconvenient for me to walk to the door to see the sign posted. It could be anything and the rage monster came out. Some of the relationships I had worked so hard to obtain in the RFCs were damaged and some were irreconcilable. It was a time filled with resentment. I felt I had every right to be mad at the world and that the world owed me something. This rage put me in a deep depression as things around me were falling apart, but yet I still felt powerful by that hatred. I felt owed by the world and that everyone around me needed to change.

I hated going to therapy. More and more was coming

up with each session. I told my therapist that I was angry all the time. I told her how much I hated my parents and how I would dream of their death. I told her the power I felt from the hate. I told her that I enjoyed thinking about how much they could suffer. I also told her that the friendships around me were suffering and of the betrayal of my best friend. I thought things were supposed to be better now that I wasn't living there anymore. Now that I wasn't getting beat all the time, but I was so wrong. Yes, things were so much better in so many ways, but they were also so difficult in so many other ways. I wanted to be like everyone else. I cried and sobbed on many occasions because I was so different. Because I couldn't form relationships like everyone else. Trust was not a word in my dictionary. I was very cautious with everyone. My acting skills never left. I knew how to evade questions and answer others with just enough truth that it would suffice everyone. I wanted relationships. I longed for close friendships and parents who loved me more than anything. I wanted a family. I wanted to belong. But mostly I wanted my family to love me and accept me. But my anger was getting in the way of everything.

I spent a lot of time in therapy talking about anger which then in turn made me more angry. I was stuck in this vicious cycle. I didn't know how to get out of it and honestly I didn't know if I wanted out of it. We talked a lot about forgiveness in therapy as well. This was simply out of the question. There was no way I was about to forgive the people who hurt me in unimaginable ways day after day after day. Despite my reactions and my adamant "No's", she kept bringing it up. With time, my heart evolved and started to open up to the idea. I was at a breaking point. I was angry at everything. My friend and I were constantly fighting. I wasn't good enough for anyone. I couldn't change fast enough for the people around me. My friend and her parents were talking about me in whispered tones. It was all falling apart. One piece at a time, but each piece felt I sunk deeper into the quicksand. Soon my head would be covered and I would be gone from everybody's life. Something had to change and that something was my stance on forgiveness.

FORGIVENESS

I THANK GOD every day for his ability to forgive us. For the ability to show us grace. I want to be more like Him in those aspects. I want to forgive more freely. I want to show grace when the rest of me is screaming to do the opposite.

I didn't understand forgiveness. You see I thought the people you were going to forgive had to apologize first. If they had apologized then I could make the decision to either forgive them or not. I thought that's how it worked, but I was so completely wrong. That's not how it works at all. You can forgive people who never apologize. You can forgive people even when they aren't remorseful. Forgiveness is a power in your hands. A power that you have to be open to. Holding onto anger is so much easier than giving into forgiveness. But forgiveness has a power far stronger than anger.

In therapy I told her I was open to the idea of forgiving my family. I just didn't know how. I also didn't really know why I needed to at the time other than her persistent encouragement to keep talking about this topic and that in the bible it says that if I don't forgive then I won't be forgiven. And man oh man I needed to be forgiven for plenty. We talked about forgiveness alongside anger for several sessions. There was a part of me that wanted to forgive them, but there was a much bigger part that turned away from this. It was a constant battle with myself. It felt like the good angel and the bad angel on my shoulders. I couldn't come to a conclusion that made sense. That worked for both sides of me. In therapy we talked about this constant struggle.

While I was going to therapy, I was still active with the RFCs. Alongside Tuesday night devos, the girls decided to do a separate devo on Thursday nights. I think this helped me along my therapy journey of changing my heart and mind. I would sit in those devos and heart that the other girls were struggling with things as well. Here I was this whole time, thinking they didn't struggle with things. They had the perfect family life. They had parents that loved them deeply and unconditionally. They had loving siblings. They had the money for school. They trusted easily and didn't have a rage monster. When I heard them open up, my eyes were opened. Oh I had plenty of struggles, but so did these girls. Each struggle was uniquely different and difficult for each person. I began to feel less isolated and more normal. The anger started to subside and my heart started to grow. I could see the anger inside of me and started to be able to pinpoint what made me angry. I started to name my anger and that took away some of the power. I began to realize that hurt people hurt people, but this was a cycle I wanted to break in myself. I was so completely hurt and broken, but I didn't want to be like my parents. I didn't want to hurt people just because I was angry. I didn't want to be a person that feasted on the weak. I didn't want my anger to fuel me. I simply didn't want to be angry. I wanted to be in control and when I was angry, I was like the Tasmanian Devil. Everything in my path was going to be destroyed. I wanted to be the complete opposite of my family. The cycle of abuse was going to stop with me. I was going to be a hurt person, who did something good for those around me. And that started with forgiveness.

I went back and forth in my mind about forgiveness. I would say one second that I forgive them and then the next I wouldn't forgive them. I would write about forgiving them and then cross it out forcefully. Like ripping the page with the pen . I would pretend to call them and tell them I forgive them and then slam the phone down. I would write a letter and then tear that letter up into tiny pieces and stomp on it. This clearly wasn't working. The only other option was to actually call them. This was the last thing I wanted to do. I absolutely hated hearing their voices. I could always tell what kind of mood they were in by their tonality and the language they used. But I knew in order for me to fully forgive them, I needed to muster up the courage and call them.

I sat in my car overlooking a park when I picked up my phone. I slid my fingers across the phone feeling the smoothness of it. I flipped it in my hand. I looked down at it wondering how this conversation was going to go. That stupid courage slowly built up and I dialed their number. I almost hung up as soon as it started ringing but I didn't know if I would go through with this again. My father picked up and I knew it was now or never. I knew I had to fight through this so that cycle could end with me. I asked him for both he and my mother to be on the line. As soon as she picked up, there was no backing out now. "I just called to say that I forgive you for all of the abuse. But just because I forgive you, do not meant that I forget what happened or that I trust you." Crickets. Then my father said, "Well we forgive you for being a horrible daughter. You only got exactly what you deserved." "I forgive you." I said and then I hung up.

I hit my steering wheel as hard as I could. Not out of anger but out of elation. I had done it! After so many months of going back and forth it was finally done. I threw my head back and just smiled. A huge sigh of relief washed over me. I was powerful. I didn't just feel powerful, but I WAS powerful. I sat in my car in pure disbelief. It didn't really even bother me what they said. I was proud of myself for staying strong and simply letting them know that I forgive them. This ginormous weight was lifted off of my shoulders. It was like the anger was lifted off of me. It was like God was wrapping His arms around me. I truly felt His presence in those moments. I was in control of my life. I had officially taken charge. Forgiving them changed everything. It was like I had just climbed Mt. Everest without oxygen and was on the peak looking at all of the beauty around me. I was in awe of what I had just done. In those few words, I took back my life. They were not going to rule me anymore. They would always be my family and they would always be part of my past, but they were not going to be part of my future. In those few words, I completely defied them. I defied them in a way they never thought was possible. I became so much stronger and vowed to do anything and everything to be the complete opposite of them. Oh the power forgiveness gave me. It was so much stronger than anger and unlike anger, I could see clearly. I wasn't exploding all over the place. I had a whole new perspective on life. A whole new since of purpose. After that phone call, I felt like I could do anything and nothing would make me upset. I felt like I could change the world. I felt free. I felt like I was floating. I was free. The anger was gone. I felt like a completely different person. A truly changed person.

Growing and Changing

As the months progressed, I came more into myself. I began to learn who I was and who I wanted to be. There was plenty that I did not like about myself and I still felt like a lot of my past was my fault. I knew I had done plenty wrong growing up and I knew that I had a smart mouth. I figured I was going to get beat anyway, so I might as well say a few things. Make the beating worth their while.

My friend and I argued a lot. We were great friends and very close but argued a lot. We played volleyball together, went on several camping and hiking trips. We would go to the movies and for ice cream. We went down to the creek and Razorback football games. We were the best of friends. We were constantly together in and out of the apartment. We would frequently go to her parents' house and go to their church functions. Their friends at church became my friends too. I spent the holidays with her family and had birthday parties with them. We were always goofing off and having a great time. I had only had one best friend before her and she ended up betraying me, so I was nervous about this relationship. That caused a lot of arguments. She was always pushing me to change something and wanted me to be farther along than I was. I was trying my best, but healing is hard. You can't just forget about what happens. And you go through the day being triggered. Some triggers you can work through fairly quickly while others stay with you all day. You can't come out of them and are stuck in the abuse. I wanted to heal faster and not have the issues I had, but it simply wasn't possible to heal at the rate she wanted.

She helped me in more ways that I could ever say. She rescued me when no one else believed me. She was there in some of the worst times. She taught me a lot about trust and not pushing people away. She showed me what a family was. As I grew, I also developed deeper relationships with her parents and sister. I began to feel more and more comfortable around them. I began to talk have conversations with them. I started joking back and forth. I wanted to spend more time with them. I wasn't as anxious to go see them and spend time with me. In fact I wanted to spend time with them whether at their house or somewhere else. To me it didn't really matter as long as I was with them.

My prayers had finally been answered. I prayed for 18-19 years for a family. For the majority of those years

I prayed for my family to be a family, but that didn't happen. But God gave me a different family and it was more than I could have ever imagined it would be. I couldn't believe this was the answer to my prayers. I now had a mom who loved me. I had a dad who wouldn't dream of hurting me. I had sisters who were protective. It was absolutely amazing! They all protected me from my biological family with a vengeance. They promised to always be there for me no matter what. I developed a trust in them. A trust that couldn't be broken.

No matter how much my friend and I fought, we always came back together. It may not have been that same day, but our friendship was unwavering. She was brutally honest to a fault but sometimes it's what I needed to hear while other times, well most of the time, it cut me deep. I didn't know how to recover from the honesty. Eventually I discovered that my arguing did little to end the argument or what she was saying. I learned that saying a small amount was better than trying to express myself. I still didn't know all of the emotions I was feeling or how to even talk about them. Or how to even attempt to say what was on my mind. Usually my words would get all twisted up and my tone was always wrong. It just escalated the argument into a full force fight. It was so much easier to just stay quiet. I was tired of being constantly wrong about things. But regardless of that, I figured it was just my fault. That I needed to change quicker and then things would be better. The fighting was exhausting but nothing like what I was used to so it was a great change in my book.

Regardless of the fighting we were still very close. She was my best friend and she saved me.

I loved this family more than anything but I didn't quite know how to navigate the family dynamics. This family was much different than my biological family. They would yell and fight and then it was over. When this happened, I would cower and freeze where I was. When her dad would suddenly get up, I would become triggered. When her mom spoke over my shoulder I would become triggered. When the door would slam I would become triggered. When someone touched my shoulder or arm or back unexpectantly I would become triggered. The moral here is that I was so very easily triggered. It didn't take much for my brain and body to be back in that abuse despite how much I had already grown and changed. Despite all of the work I had done the triggers and flash-backs continued. Finding my place within this already established family was difficult. I didn't know how to do the many things that everyone else already knew how to do. I didn't know how to cook or sew. I didn't know how to act when other people came over to the house. I didn't know how to react in different situations or what to say. I didn't know how much to be out with everyone and how much time to let them be a family. Family dynamics were a constant struggle, but I finally had my family. I finally had the answer to my prayers. To the sleepless nights of begging and pleading with God. I was happy. I was where I was supposed to be. I was with the people God had planned for me to be with. I was so happy. My life was coming together in ways I didn't think were possible.

I continued therapy off and on after I made the step to forgive my family. It wasn't something I felt like I needed to continue on a regular basis because I was doing much better. I wasn't the angry individual I once was. Despite therapy helping, I felt so ashamed to go. I felt like the people who knew I went looked down on me. Like I was this broken person and they didn't believe therapy would actually do any good. I felt like they saw me as someone beyond help. I felt judged by going to therapy. I felt like I was a lesser person because I couldn't fix things on my own. I had this thought and belief that I should be fine. I wasn't living with my biological family anymore so I should be fine. I shouldn't have to go to therapy. I felt much better than I had and in my book that was enough. So therapy became a hit of miss type of thing. When things started to spiral off track then I would go back for a few sessions and then stop again. My friend continually pushed for me to go back to therapy each time that I stopped going, but she wasn't the one having to go through the torment of therapy. The torment of driving there and getting out of the car and then actually talking. She didn't experience the torment of my past so I didn't really listen to what she had to say regarding therapy anymore. I wanted to be in charge of myself. I knew myself better than she did even though she boasted to know me better.

I depended on her for many things. I depended on her to show me what a family truly was. I depended on her to be on my side and see things from my point of view. I depended on her to support me and encourage me along the way. I depended on her to always be there no matter what. We were as close as you could get. She was more than my best friend; she was my sister. She was the only person there for me when I didn't have anybody at all. I can't describe how close we were and how much I looked up to her. I took everything she said to heart. I believed every word that came out of her mouth. If she said it, the it must be true. Who was I to argue with her? She grew up with a loving family. She grew up without abuse and trauma at every turn. She grew up stable and secure. She grew up being able to express herself and learned how to express herself appropriately. She grew up with a level head. She grew up with confidence and self-esteem. She was the popular kid and had the outgoing, bubbly personality. She was everything that I wanted to be. She truly had it all. She was my person through thick and thin.

When she got accepted to Harding University for her masters, I couldn't understand why she would want to go there. It was such a horrible place for me and she was welcoming it with open arms. It turned out to be great for her, but with each visit, more of my past came back to haunt me. Not only that, but my roommate had left and I had to navigate everything on my own. This would be the first time I lived on my own since moving to Fayetteville. I moved a lot during this time. I was also finishing school and trying to save as much money as possible for grad school applications. This time alone was nothing short of lonely. I didn't know who to turn to. My best friend was gone and talking to her just wasn't the same. Even when we hung out, it wasn't the same. It was like some of our closeness just evaporated when she went to Harding. She didn't come visit me in Fayetteville so if I wanted to see her, I had to go to Searcy, AR (that's where Harding is). This small thing became a large crack in our friendship. She was still the closest friend I had by far, but it didn't seem like I was her closest friend anymore. Trips and visits would be planned and then canceled. I had to drive to a place that had very few good memories just to see my friend. I didn't feel important to her anymore. I felt like I was just something that was easy to throw away. Like I didn't matter to her anymore.

During the time she was at Harding, I would spend more time with her family. I longed to be close to the family in some sort of fashion. But I realized that the trips they made to Fayetteville were based around my friend, and not me. They didn't come to Fayetteville to visit anymore. I had to go down to see them. I began to feel left out of everything. Things were evolving and changing while I was left on the outskirts watching it happen. I began to make less frequent trips to see them and would just call my friends mom every week instead. I desperately wanted to be important in their lives. I didn't want to be this burden or this thing for them to just check off of their list. I wanted to be a full member of the family, but it was becoming more and more obvious that I was not that in their lives.

I became deeply depressed. I only had enough money

to apply to one grad school so I took the chance to apply to the University of Arkansas. I figured this was my best bet since the teachers already knew me. They knew my situation as to why schooling took me longer than it should have. They also knew I wasn't good at taking tests, but I knew the material. I was on pins and needles waiting for the letter to come in the mail. If I didn't get into grad school there wasn't anything I could have done with my degree. I would have wasted all of my time and stressed myself out about schooling for no reason. I felt added pressure with the family dynamics. I thought that if I got accepted to grad school then I would be important enough for them to come see me. I also always felt like I was competing with my friend. She was naturally smart and didn't have to study often to make As on everything. Whereas I would study for hours and would rarely make As on tests. She was always scoring higher than me in everything and I wanted for once to be good at something the first time.

The letter came in the mail. I was filled with excitement and anxiety. I prayed I would be accepted. I didn't have any back up plans. My future was determined by what this letter said. I took a deep breath and opened it. My eyes immediately filled with tears as I read over the words, "We regret to inform you that you have not been accepted into the graduate program for Communication Disorders at the University of Arkansas." I was devastated! I fell back onto the couch clutching that letter hoping the words would change with each time I read it. Once again my plans failed and I didn't know what else to do. I was supposed to go to grad school. That was the next step, but now where that step should have been was a giant crater. I fell into a deep depression. The crack in my friendship widened and my place in the family continued to grow more confusing. I didn't want to be around anyone or do anything. I believed the words of my parents once again with full force. "You will never amount to anything. You aren't good for anything. Nobody will ever love you. You will never have a family. You will always tear people down. You are the problem in everything. You shouldn't exist. You are a nothing and a nobody." I couldn't get their words out of my head. I couldn't think straight. I was so completely lost. That letter sent me in a downward spiral faster than a sinking rock.

COMPLETELY LOST

AFTER GETTING THAT letter, I still had to go back to school and face those professors who denied my acceptance. I had to hear my friends talking about grad school and where they got accepted. With each passing day I grew more and more depressed. What was I going to do? My friends were al so very excited and their lives were going in the right direction. They weren't taking leaps backwards but doing what they were sup0posed to be doing. Why couldn't I be like them? Why couldn't I be happy too? Why couldn't my life be going in the right direction for once? I was completely shattered. I didn't even tell my friend or her family for weeks after I got the letter. I knew they were not going to be shocked by the outcome. I knew I was amounting up to be nobody. I knew their prime focus was my friend and her sister and not me. They said the loved me but I didn't see it and I sure didn't feel it. The words which were said to me were not very encouraging and I didn't find any comfort in them. I didn't want to show my face to them. I knew I was a disappointment and I just couldn't bear it. I spent a lot of time in my apartment by myself. I was so completely lonely. I wanted to have friends and people over but I also couldn't bear the thought of being around anybody. My world had gone from hopeful and moving forward to a very, very dark place all because of 23 words.

GRADUATION

As DARK AS my world had become, I had come up with a plan. My boss had agreed to hire me full-time at the day care as soon as I graduated. I wasn't going to go to grad school this year but I could spend the year studying for the GRE and saving up my money for applications for next year. It was really all that I could do. So my world was still dark but more of a light gray than pitch black.

Graduation was upon me and I was so extremely happy. My family had all come in for the event as well as some special friends. I had defied the odds. I had survived the abuse. I had found a way to get back into school. I had found a way to pay for that schooling and now I was graduating with my bachelor's in communication disorders. I had done it! I had help along the way, but I made it to graduation. A day I didn't think was ever going to happen.

A day I had only dreamed about for so long, but now my dream had become my reality.

Everything was perfect! Everyone I loved and cared about was there. They drove just to see me graduate. I was outside with all of my friends from my program in our caps and gowns and then it happened. He walked up and stopped right in front of me. He was my father carrying a bouquet of flowers. *They are here! Why did they have to come? This is MY day! I don't want to share this day with them or their drama. Why did they have to come? Why couldn't they have just left me alone? They keep saying they love me, but if they truly loved me then they should have stayed away. I just want to have one special day. I have to call my friend. I need to borrow a phone, but I can't let him see me. Move body! Move! But slowly! Don't draw attention to yourself. Act normal and not like a murder is standing right in front of you.* I slowly turned in a way, where I could see him out of the corner of my eye and asked to borrow a phone. I called my friend and told her they were here and I needed to know where they were sitting. I didn't want to look directly at them as I walked in or out because I knew they would be calling my name. I went from sheer happiness to complete anxiety in just a few seconds. I needed the information and I needed it quickly. My friend was able to call back and let me know where my biological family was sitting. He stayed out there until it was almost time for us to walk in. *Stay calm Suzanne. We have a plan in place on how to get me out of here without them getting their hands on me. This is my day. I worked hard for this day.*

I have come too far to let them ruin this. I vowed right then and there that I was just going to act like I hadn't even seen him. Like nothing had changed. I was graduating for goodness sake and nothing and nobody was going to ruin that!

When we were walking in, I could hear them call my name several times. My friends said my family was yelling for me so I turned my head toward their direction, waved and smiled at some people in the back row. They were on the first row. I spotted my friends family further down the stadium and kept my eyes on the people who actually cared about me. After I passed my biological family, I forgot they were even there. I pushed it so far back and just enjoyed the ceremony. Now I have no idea who spoke or what they said, but I remember being there with my friends. I remember talking to them. I remember my name being called and the sense of pride the devoured me as I walked across that stage.

When we walked out and were coming up the ramp, I noticed my friends dad at the top. Now this was not according to the plan we had laid out so I knew something must be wrong. I gave him a hug and he gently pushed me to the side of him while he continued walking forward and had his arm wrapped tightly around me. He said we can hug later. Plans have changed and I'm taking you to the car. I said to him that there was no way we were going to get to the car before my biological family got to me. He said yes there is and at that moment my friend pulled up at the curb. Her dad pushed me into the car and we drove off. I looked out the window and there was my father half walking and half jogging to find me. Not only had I graduated, but I had done so without them getting their hands on me. Our meeting place was behind the RFC building. I remember getting out and giving my friend the biggest hug I had ever given because she once again protected me and saved me. I was also filled with a joy that is indescribable.

It wasn't until late that night when all of the celebrating was over that the reality of it really hit me. The reality of how close I was to being back in their clutches. And the reality of how truly sad I was that instead of being happy that my family was there, I was filled with dread and anxiety. It hit me how sad it was and how sad I was. I heard their sad voices when I walked out past them and didn't look at them. It hit me how much I had hurt them. Despite everything they had done, I still loved them. It's a weird kind of love. I wanted them to be proud and maybe they were when I graduated. Maybe they were truly happy and just wanted to celebrate and didn't have any ulterior motives. I will never know. I just remember being heartbroken that I didn't want them there and then that I had hurt them. I didn't ever want to hurt them after I finally forgave them. The thought didn't cross my mind anymore and instead of wishing for them to hurt, I felt sorry for them. I wanted to share in the joy I was feeling with them, but I also knew how bad of an idea that was. This didn't send me into a depression, but it did start some questioning. I wondered if I should have left them. I wondered if I should have cut ties with them. I wondered if I was doing the right thing by listening and following the advice of my friends family. I wondered if the advice they were giving me was good advice. I wondered if I should go back to my family. I wondered if God hated me for the decisions I had made. I wondered if I would go to Hell because I didn't honor my mother and father.

Graduation was the first time I had seen them in a long time and it brought up a lot of feelings. I wanted with all of my being to run into my father's arms like I had when I was a very little girl. I loved the idea of my family. I loved the idea of my family loving me, but it just wasn't my reality. I wanted to be with them. I wanted to be with the good memories of them. Not the people who I had to fear. I loved my friends family, but the relationship I had with her mom was not the same relationship her mom had with her daughters. The relationship I had with her dad wasn't the same relationship her dad had with his daughters. It just wasn't the same. It wasn't the close relationship I longed for. I wasn't looked at the same way. I was looked at as lesser than and it was devastating to me, but it was the closest thing I was going to get to the real thing. So many times I brushed off these feelings and just moved on, but it still hurt seeing the relationships they had with their daughters.

Maybe, Just Maybe

I SPENT A lot of time in prayer over the next year while my life was at a standstill. Work was wonderful. I had more responsibility and became the full-time pre-k teacher. Other people were seeing potential in me that I didn't see. Other people saw me amounting up to something that I couldn't see. Over the next year, I spent a lot of time in nature. I have always loved being outside but having to navigate through this period in my life on my own, nature was special. It allowed me to see things more clearly. It allowed me to focus and to really set some good stepping stones in place for my life. I wanted to be with other people, but I was also finding that I was capable of being by myself and finding things to do on my own. It was a chance for me to experience things in a way I never had before. I spent a lot of time studying for the GRE and fretting over grad school and money. I became pretty frugal with my money because I knew I would have to take the test multiple times and that each application was pricy. During this year away from school I kept int contact with one professor in particular who suggested a little university in Tahlequah, Oklahoma. She thought it would be a perfect fit for me and even gave me the contact information for a professor in the Communication Disorders/Speech-Language Pathology department. I knew I needed all of the help I could get so I jumped on the opportunity. I called the professor at Northeastern State University and set up an interview and campus visit.

I immediately fell in love with the town and the area. It was beautiful. The Illinois River was there, a creek ran through town and Lake Tenkiller was just a few short miles away. There were rolling hills, winding roads, and hiking everywhere you turned. I prayed to get accepted. The interview went great and I knew when my application went across their desks they would have a face and a personality to go with that application. They would have a story to go with that piece of paper. It was all that I could do.

When time came to put in my applications, I was able to put in for 5 or 6 this time, but there was really only one school I wanted to go to. I didn't know if I was going to be able to handle another round of rejections. I knew I didn't add up to the other people applying. It was a very competitive field, but I knew if I could just get accepted I could prove my worth. I could prove that I was worth the chance. I just needed to get in. The letters started coming in one by one. "We regret to inform you that you have not been accepted into the graduate program for Communication Disorders at the XYZ University." With each letter my hope dissipated. I was going to be stuck as pre-k teacher at a day care for the rest of my life. It was a great job but it wasn't what I wanted to do. It wasn't the vision I had for my life. I had planned for more, but all of my plans failed no matter what preparation I did. No matter how much detail I gave every plan. They always fell through. My hope was gone. I hadn't even gotten a letter from Northeastern State University. Then weeks later I opened the mailbox to see a letter from Northeaster State University. Every other university had rejected me. I hoped it wouldn't be the case with this one, but I didn't have much hope. This was my last chance.

I set the letter down on my table and made some food. I couldn't bring myself to open the letter. I was so afraid that it would just be another rejection letter and I couldn't bear the bad news. I couldn't bear my family being right about me after all of these years. I ate and then watched TV. If I didn't see those same stupid words then the rejection couldn't happen. It was like sweeping it under the rug.

I finally picked up that letter and just held it in my hand. *Please accept me. Please let me in. I have no other plan. Please just take a chance on me. Just let me prove to you that I belong. Please, please, please just let me in.* I turned the envelope over and closed my eyes. I slowly tore it open and centimeter by centimeter I pulled the letter out. "We congratulate you on your acceptance into the graduate program for Speech-Language Pathology at Northeastern State University." *WHAT?!?!?!!?!?!?!* I re-read that first sentence several times. It never changed! It continued to say that I was ACCEPTED!!!!! I jumped up and down screaming, shouting, whooping and hollering. Northeastern State University was my last shot and they took a chance on me.

Moving Forward

I BEGAN PACKING and making living arrangements almost immediately. I let everyone know I was going to grad school. That my life was finally moving forward. But moving day came, and I got so sick. This would be my first true time on my own. Even when I went to Harding, I knew people that were there. When I moved to Fayetteville I had friends there. When I moved to Tahlequah, I didn't know a single soul. There was not one person I knew from there. I discovered later on that a fellow RFC was from there and he became my go-to guy during my time down there. He showed me around and showed me the best kept secrets. He came to my rescue with my car countless times and helped me find a mechanic. He even made sure the mechanic didn't upcharge a single female who knew nothing about cars.

But see I didn't know that he was from Tahlequah at the time that I was moving there. It wasn't until later that I discovered this. I was scared. I was nervous. I was anxious. I was sick to my stomach. I was leaving my home. I was leaving the family I had found. I was leaving all of my friends and my church. I was leaving behind all of those feelings you get of home. I was leaving everything behind. I had never had a home before Fayetteville. I had changed so much during my time there. I had grown. I had overcome obstacles. I had graduated. I had forgiven my family there. I had grown and changed and become someone so different during my time there. Fayetteville was the best thing to ever happen to me and I couldn't imagine leaving. And my stomach couldn't imagine it either. As we were getting to the last items to load up, I locked myself in the bathroom feeling so completely nauseous. The tears started to fall and I couldn't catch my breath. My friend was mad at me for not helping load up my own stuff, but I didn't think I could get off of the floor nor could I stop the tears. She thought it was ridiculous that I was acting like this, but I don't think she ever realized what Fayetteville meant to me.

Eventually everything was loaded and we were on our way. I knew that my friends family would just drive there, help unload and then go back home. I knew that in a matter of hours I was truly going to be on my own. If something happened I had no help. I had no one to turn to. I had nobody and I was terrified. I remember the last items being brought into my cute little apartment and then saying good-bye. They all said they would come visit but I honestly didn't believe it. Especially after what happened when my friend left to go to Harding. I knew they meant well, but it was just hard for me to believe. When they pulled out of the apartment I looked around, saw all of my stuff and just cried. There was no turning back. I was more alone than I have ever felt. I had no desire to unpack anything. I just sat and cried for hours.

It was a new beginning and I was either going to thrive or fail horribly. The next day I began to unpack and decided that Northeastern State University took a chance on me, so I needed to take a chance on me too. I needed to see what I could do completely on my own. Away from everyone I knew. It was a clean slate for me and I was going to do all that I could to make myself proud.

GRAD SCHOOL

AND SO IT began. For the next two years of my life I would be in school and I was going to make them the best two years of my life. I walked into my first class filled with apprehension, anxiety, happiness, and appreciation. These professors hand picked me to be here studying. I was honored. I was humbled. I was also a little older than the other people in my class. I was shocked at how easy the material came to me. I always struggled in undergrad and had to study all the time just to make decent grades, but that wasn't the case here. The material was easier for me to understand with the exception of statistics but math and I have never gotten along. Maybe it was the fact that I had worked in day care for 5 years and full time for the last year, but I just understood the development of kids. I understood what was normal and what wasn't. I absorbed the information my professors were teaching like a sponge and retained it all. I didn't have to try to prove myself, I already was.

Looking back, I am so thankful that I was a grad school reject. I am so thankful that all of those school rejected me and only Northeastern State University (NSU) took a chance on me. If I hadn't gotten into NSU then I wouldn't have met the best teacher I have ever had. Not only was she an exceptional teacher, she was a phenomenal mother and role model. She was unlike anyone I had ever known. She was true. She was genuine. She was real. She didn't have ulterior motives. She didn't look at me like a broken person after I opened up to her like everyone else had. She instilled confidence in me. She had a way of teaching where you didn't feel criticized.

Grace made my life so much better in every way. My family only came down for one visit and it was right before I started school. They came down to visit me for my birthday. It was a truly wonderful day and I was so shocked that they came. I was so thankful they came, but they didn't come again. Despite being only about an hour or so away, they didn't come. My best friend was even closer than that, but she didn't come either. It was becoming clearer and clearer that coming to see me wasn't on their agenda. It wasn't something they felt drawn to do. They were drawn to drive to see their daughters wherever they were, but not their extra daughter regardless of where she was. It became apparent that if I wanted to spend time with anybody in my family then I would have to make the effort and this tugged on my heart. It made me feel less than. It discouraged me. It made me begin to question a lot about them and a lot about my biological family. I started to wonder if they were that much different. I began to feel like they were avoiding me on purpose.

But Grace was so different. During a time that I was questioning a lot, she showed me family. She invited me to her family functions. She invited me, a grad student, a reject, into her home and introduced me to all of her family. And instantly I knew this is what family was. There was so much love and giving. There weren't favorites or ulterior motives. There was love. And I couldn't get enough of it.

It's hard to describe a feeling of people accepting you fully and without judgement. Of accepting you without looking at you like you are broken. It was unlike anything I had ever felt. It was beautiful. It was life changing. I felt like I was part of her family.

I continued to blossom in my program. For the first time in my life I was getting straight A's. I felt a confidence that I didn't know I could even possess. During clinicals I was praised by professors and guardians of my clients. I was shocked at my abilities and the praises I was receiving. I was in awe of the written notes on my evaluation sheets (I still have these and look at them from time to time). For the first time in my life I was truly good at something. For the first time in my life I was changing lives. For the first time in my life I was truly happy for extended periods of time. I had found a happiness and a sense of purpose. I wasn't a nobody, but I was a somebody. That didn't just come because I was making good grades or was good at clinicals. It came because of the love Grace and her family showed me. It came because she believed in me and her belief changed the belief I had in myself.

I didn't have to question what I was doing at night. I wasn't alone unless I wanted to be. I had found a home in Grace and her family. A true home. Where yes, they loved their daughters, but they loved me too. There wasn't this picking and choosing like I had experienced before. I asked for my friends family and my friend to come down on several occasions. I wanted to introduce them. I wanted to show them the beauty of Tahlequah. I wanted them to see how well I was doing. I wanted them to be part of my life.

I realized there are several different families and sometimes some mean well, but don't quite have the follow through. My friends family was special in so many ways. They were wonderful in so many ways. They loved in their own way, but it was hard for them to fully accept me. Grace's family on the other hand was what I thought family really was supposed to be. I thought I had found that in my friends family, but once I met Grace's it was this Ah-ha moment. A smile spread across my face and it just didn't leave. I felt at peace with them. I felt at ease. I didn't feel judged or that I had to do so many things right in order to gain their love and attention. When God says to love, that's what this family did. They never wavered. They never stopped. Showing love was as natural as breathing to them. There was this calming peace and full embodiment of joy that came over me when I was with them. It was intoxicating and addicting. If this was a drug I would have paid top dollar for it. Grace and her family were a true blessing. A blessing I didn't realize I even needed. They were everything to me. They filled me with such confidence. Grace filled me with confidence at school, but outside of school they all had this ability to encourage and guide without arrogance. They had this ability to see beyond who you wanted people to see and to see the true you. I never felt like I had to act around them. I could let my guard down and the city fortress I had built around me. What they said was truth, honest, loving truth. I had never experienced such love, such true love before. It is a feeling I can't describe, but a feeling I can never forget.

My whole time I was in Tahlequah I experienced the generosity of this family. I was free to show up unannounced and stay as long as I wanted. This family showed me the type of person I wanted to be and helped me to grow in that direction.

I had absolutely no desire to get married or to have kids. But that changed with the more time I spent with them. I saw a loving marriage. I saw a dad who was fiercely protective of his daughters, and me. I saw a man who loved his wife and showered her with love. I saw a man who not only spoke love but showed it to all those around him. I saw a man who provided for his family.

I saw a grandfather who deeply supported his grandchildren in everything they did. I saw a grandfather who was God on earth. He so passionately loved everyone. I witnessed his face completely light up when his daughters walked in the room. I saw a man who loved his wife and cherished every moment with her. I felt the loving strength from him with each and every hug. I saw him spread the love of God like he was Santa Clause passing out gifts. I saw a wise man who you could not help but stop and listen to.

I saw a mom who cherished her daughters. I saw a mom who deeply loved those around her. I saw a mom who was protective of her daughters, and me. I saw a mom who saw her daughters as a miracle, as a blessing, as a gift from God. I saw a woman who loved her husband and continually showed him. I saw a woman who put God first and just barely under that was her family. I saw a woman who got pure joy from her family.

I saw two daughters who were so uniquely beautiful. They were so different but yet so much the same. I saw two daughters who knew how special their parents were. I saw two daughters who loved God. I saw two daughters who had everything in the world. I saw two daughters that knew how different their lives could have been without their mom and dad.

I saw a family so in love with God and each other. I saw a family unlike any other family I have ever witnessed. And I saw a family that accepted me. A family who could have turned their backs on me. A family that could have said, you can't come to our house or to our daughters events. A family who could have said no, but instead said yes. A family that I am so grateful for. A family that is a true family.

My eyes began to open to the possibility of marriage and the possibility of children. Now that I knew what it could look like, that's what I wanted. If I could be just a smidge like them, I would count it as a success. My eyes and heart opened up in ways that I thought my heart was so completely closed off to, but now it was cut wide open.

I cannot say enough about how Grace and her family changed me. Their love and support got me through extremely difficult times. Knowing I had a place to go to. Knowing I had a face to see. Knowing I had someone(s) who truly loved me, made all the difference in the world. I changed so much in the two years I was in Tahlequah. Grace and her family molded me and instilled in me values I didn't have before. They instilled in me a self-confidence which I will forever be grateful for. They instilled in me what it meant to live like Christ. They instilled in me a sense of belonging. They gave me a family.

WHAT A POSSIBILITY

WHILE I WAS in Tahlequah, I tried to be part of a campus ministry, but honestly after being an RFC, this campus ministry was depressing. It was so small and nobody was really into it. But I would still do things with them when I wasn't with Grace and her family. It was here in this small campus ministry that I met a friend. He was just a goofy guy and we had fun together. It wasn't anything serious at all. Literally just friends. And then one day a mutual friend said to me, "You know he likes you right?!" *What? She must be crazy!* "And you know that you are flirting with him right?!" *Oh see now I know she must be crazy!* "No way" I said. "We are just friends hanging out." "There is nothing more to it." I didn't for a second believe what she was saying. We were just hanging out. That was it. But now I began to second guess everything. I closely watched what he did and how he said things. I also began to watch what I said and did. As I watched more closely, I became more and more nervous with each interaction. I wasn't even looking for a guy. I wasn't completely closed off to the idea anymore, but I also wasn't completely open to it either. I was navigating uncharted waters for sure. What started out as a friendship slowly grew into something a little more.

When we started being more serious, he was graduating with his undergraduate degree. He then moved about an hour away for postgraduate. We spent a lot of time together both in Tulsa and in Tahlequah as our relationship blossomed. I was feeling things I had never felt before. My eyes were seeing things through a different lense. A void which I didn't know I had was being filled by his love. Oh there was healing in his love. There was comfort when we our fingers were intertwined. There was a newness in my life I was so very thankful for. I loved spending every second with him. The majority of our relationship was long distance and for somebody who was trying to figure out if this is what I wanted or not, this worked out well. It gave me a chance to evaluate our relationship and honestly for me to miss him.

At this point and time in my life I had become quite independent. I loved only having myself to think about (what to do for fun, what to eat, what movie to see, etc.). The idea of marriage scared me. There was such a fear associated with this. With opening up my heart in this way. I would be vulnerable in so many ways, but my heart couldn't help but to fall in love with him. And believe me, I tried to not fall in love. I went for a while trying to find every fault he had just to make sure I didn't fall in love. But it didn't work. I fell head over heels in love. He was funny. He was cute. His kisses were sweet and soft. He would kiss me on the forehead (which come on girls, you all know you love that). He would open the door for me. He took things at my pace. He was patient and kind and loving. He was more than I could have ever imagined. Oh how my love grew. I looked forward to each visit and despised when we had to say good-bye. I loved how I felt in his arms and how safe he made me feel. I loved how he loved me.

I couldn't believe this was happening. I was fully in love with this guy. Despite every effort I made, he crept his way into my heart. I couldn't imagine my life without him, but I was still nervous about marriage. I was afraid of being that close to a guy. Of being that vulnerable. Of being intimate. I constantly argued with myself about giving into the love regardless of the fear. I couldn't believe this girl who wasn't supposed to amount to anything, was now fully in love with this wonderful guy. The girl who almost died, is now thriving. Marriage was now a possibility and not just a dream. It wasn't something that I just wanted in theory, but something that was eventually going to happen with this guy. I became deeply attached to his family while I was falling so madly in love with him. I never knew love could feel so good.

As graduation draw closer so did the job hunt. I was

ready to graduate, but at the same time I didn't want to. I didn't want to leave Grace and her family and Tahlequah behind. I didn't want to leave behind this happiness which I had found. I didn't want to leave behind this family which accepted regardless of my past. I didn't want to leave and start all over again, but at the same time, I was ready to start all over again. I was ready to put everything I learned into practice. I was ready for my school caseload (I just never fully realized just how big that caseload was going to be).

Moving.....Again

IF THERE IS one constant in my life it is moving. I have frequently joked about starting my own moving company. I wasn't ever good at geometry in school but give me a stack of items to be loaded into a moving van or a vehicle and I've got you covered.

After a serious contemplation about moving to Alaska, I ended up staying in Oklahoma and moved to a town about an hour away. This now meant that I was now a little over 2 hours away from the man I was so deeply in love with. Now you've got to realize that during this time, I was giving into fully loving him. I was still apprehensive at times, yes, but his love felt so incredibly good. I was told that my eyes said everything. The way I looked at him was different. There was awe and longing in my eyes when I looked at him. There was a peace that I had when I was with him. There were several times where I had to tell myself that this was real. That I wasn't just making this up.

My friends family all approved of him. I asked them to specifically look for red flags and let me know. I was so fearful of tying the knot and being vowed to someone for the rest of my life who was going to turn out to be just like my biological family. I pushed them to find something, so that I could be 100% certain that this was the guy for me. That this was the guy I could have a family with. This was the guy who was going to be my happily ever after.

They found nothing. Not a single thing. My friend instantly became close with him and viewed him as a brother. They just instantly clicked. My friends family all absolutely adored him. He could do no wrong in their eyes. I was amazed that I had found a guy who they approved of. Who they didn't find any faults with. Who they loved. I was so incredibly happy.

Moving Fast

It all happened so fast, and so slow at the same time. He and I greatly enjoyed hiking and exploring new areas. Nature and I have a special relationship. In some ways, I felt closer to him while we were out in nature. Experiencing the awe of what God had created from the miniscule blades of grass to the vast growth and depth of the trees. It was on one of these hikes where he proposed. I was in the lead and there was a sign which said, "Turn Around". Without suspecting anything at all, I turned around, and there he was down on one knee. Oh it was beautiful. It was magnificent. It was more than I could ever dream of. The man I loved with all of my heart was there proposing to me. He was the most handsome thing I had ever seen. I was filled with giddy joy and continued to look at him and that ring on my finger. And man oh man did that ring on my finger look good. I was so incredibly happy. I didn't even know happiness like this existed. I thought it was only reserved for fairy tales.

For the next couple of months my friends family hounded me about a date. I didn't want it to be a fast engagement. I wanted to savor it. I knew I didn't want a big wedding at all so setting a date wasn't important to me. I wanted to get married, but honestly I wasn't in any sort of rush. Also now that this ring was on my finger the apprehension and anxieties began to creep up. I knew with marriage that meant sex and I wasn't too fond of this. I knew it was something he craved and wanted but it wasn't something I had healed from.

Setting a date meant setting the date for the wedding night. I wasn't prepared to face that. Oh part of me longed to have sex with him, while the other part could only remember and relive the past traumas. I finally got tired of the constant hounding about a date and we set one in play, just 5 months after we were engaged. In my book, this wasn't ideal, but when it came to my friend and her family, I didn't have the confidence to stick up for myself. I loved them dearly and they are great people but arguing from my point of view never did any good. We kept coming back to the same argument until I conceded.

Now that the date was set in play everything else had to quickly be arranged. Mind you I am at my first job with my degree carrying a huge caseload and trying to navigate this whole new world. While I got engaged and was planning a wedding. It was a lot. There wasn't much time to breathe or to take things in.

I wasn't the girl who thought about her wedding throughout her childhood. Who had an idea of what she wanted. I was the girl who said second by second *How am I going to survive this?* Anything down the road, any planning was completely out of the question growing up. I had to take things second by second just to make sure I wasn't six feet under. So thinking about my wedding was completely out of the question. It was something I had determined years ago wasn't going to happen. If I made it out, I wasn't ever going to allow another guy to hurt me like my father and my brother. I wasn't going to be a mother because I had no earthly idea how to be one. Mine sure showed me what not to do, but I didn't know what I was supposed to do. These things in my life were shut down from a very early age. So now that I was sitting in this position with a ring on my finger and a guy looking at me with deep love in his eyes, was almost more than I could take in. It was a time of extreme mixed emotions and I wasn't able to express them adequately. I believe that if I had been able to , then my friend and her family would understand my apprehension.

So now I'm getting questions left and right about the wedding. Colors, location, cakes, invitations, engagement pictures, honeymoon, money, decorations, guest list, etc from every angle. I couldn't process it all. I couldn't figure out what I wanted. All I knew was that I didn't want my father, mother, or brother to know or be there. I did; however, want my grandmother there who was living with my aunt and uncle to be at the reception. I knew that I didn't want a big wedding. I didn't want all of that attention on me. I didn't care about having a reception afterward, but I didn't want that many people there at the actual wedding. I didn't even mind wearing my wedding dress to the reception so people could see it. I had decided that I didn't want a typical wedding dress. I didn't want to go through all of the fittings and I didn't want to spend a lot of money on a dress or anything for that matter. I just wanted a simple white dress that I could wear again if I so chose to. I ended up buying my simple off white, lacy, shin length dress online. When it came in, it was everything I wanted. It fit me perfectly and was marvelous. I could care less about the rest of the plans. I had my dress and the guy. What else did I need? But the questions kept pouring in. My friend and her mom became increasingly upset with me because of how nonchalant I was being. I honestly didn't care about the details. As long as her dad would marry me and this amazing guy, I was perfectly fine. I didn't need anything else. I really didn't care about rest of the details. We decided upon a location that I knew would be beautiful and yes of course it was outside.

As the wedding date drew closer and closer the more nervous I became. I wasn't nervous to marry him; I was nervous at what marriage would entail. I was nervous for that wedding night. I didn't think I could go through with it, but who was I going to talk to about this dilemma? I knew it was something I would have to get over because it was my job to please the man. At least that's what I was told and what I fully believed. When I said I do, I was to be submissive to him in all ways. And I knew that involved sex. And I knew I had to figure this out. I just wanted for my love to be enough for him. I knew his love would be enough for me.

Starting A New Life

THE WEDDING WAS perfect. There weren't very many people there. My man looked so handsome. The weather was perfect. And the ceremony was less than 10 minutes. Perfection. After a celebratory lunch, it was time to say our goodbyes as our life was now starting. I was overcome with emotion. The tears fell freely. I was in awe that I had amounted to something. I had gotten through school and grad school and was now working using my degree. I had a real family in my friends family. I found a wonderful, godly man who I fell so in love with and now I am married. I was also sad, that I was now leaving everything behind that I knew. Every relationship would change and nothing in my world would be the same again. I was so happy to have my happily ever after, but I knew with that happily ever after, sex would be a big part of it. And sex had proved to only be traumatizing. It had only proved to me that the guy took what he wanted. I knew this man loved me, but the longing for that ecstasy would take over at some point if I didn't give it to him.

I will spare you the details but the wedding night came and it went. There are no details because nothing happened. I couldn't get over my fear. I couldn't get over the flashbacks that were haunting me. Oh how I longed for it to happen, but it just didn't. We would be flying to Mexico in the next day or two and then the honeymoon would really start. I figured I would have it all figured out by that time. There was such pressure on me because I knew this was what I was supposed to do. I knew I told him once we were married it would happen, but I couldn't get out of my head. I knew my friend would be asking and I couldn't stand when I let her down. I would be lettering her down and my new husband all at the same time and it was too much for me to handle.

Mexico was beautiful and so was my new husband. I loved getting to be there with him and experiencing this with him. I even swept the little lies he told under the rug. I was so happy and it was so beautiful. I was so in love. Now I am the type of person that when you go somewhere, you explore. You cram in as much as you possibly can because the chance of getting to go back is so slim. This was my thought process. I wanted to see and explore. I figured we would just have sex at night after we have explored together throughout the day. This was not his idea and I don't know about your idea of a honeymoon, but you may tend to agree with him. I wanted to be with him in every capacity, but the traumas kept coming up. He knew about some of the trauma but always thought that once we were married, it would just flow naturally. This was far from the case and it quickly made him frustrated. Regardless of the anxiety on my part and the frustration on his, we still had a wonderful time in Mexico. It's a time I wouldn't dare trade for anything. It was a time where we grew closer. It was a time where I realized I had to let my friend go and make him my priority. It was a time when I realized he was now my best friend. It was a time filled to the brim with laughter and smiles. It was a time of strangers congratulating us and feeling like we were so incredibly special. It was a time where I felt comfortable with being wrapped in his arms and showing it off in public. It was a time where I was so truly, deeply, madly in love and never wanted to leave. I only wanted to be with him. It was a time of giddiness and joy and love. It was a time when my face was sore every night from smiling and laughing so much.

All too quickly we had to go back home. I was so sad to leave. I knew once we got back home, we were going to have to part ways. He still had to pack up before he could move in with me. Going back meant back to reality and I just wasn't ready for that. When we got back into the states we had to say goodbye. This goodbye was so much harder than I had anticipated. I think partly because he was already supposed to be packed and was supposed to be moving into my townhouse the next day. Instead everything got pushed back by a couple of weeks.

We had a wonderful reception the next weekend. Anybody who wanted to come was welcome. I wore my dress and he wore his suit. This is where we did everything you normally would at a reception. So many people came including my grandmother and aunt and uncle. This would be one of my last memories with my grandmother before the Alzheimer's took over. It was such a time of celebration. I was so happy that so many people whom I loved could be there to share in the joy.

FINALLY TOGETHER

IT TOOK LONGER than it should have, but we were finally living together. He had moved in with me since I was on contract and would not dissolve it. During this time, he was not attending grad school so it made perfect sense for him to move in with me. Things were different. They were strange. They were good. They were weird. Having a boy live with you when you have become so independent required quite the learning curve. We both very much loved one another, but we were a long distance relationship. Not the relationship that gets together every day. So in a way we had to learn each other all over again. In a way that was uniquely different than before.

Throughout this time I was deeply struggling, but I didn't want to show him that. I wanted to be the perfect wife. I put pressure on myself. I listened to my friend and her mom when I sought advice. I was struggling with being fully submissive. You see submissive for me equates to trauma. I always had to be submissive to my abusers. I always had to be submissive so they could get what they wanted while I was left high and dry. Submissiveness was bloodcurdling terrifying for me. I contacted my therapist who I had seen off and on, but never once while I was in Tahlequah. We agreed to some sessions and then she wanted to bring in my husband so we could work some things out. I needed the help in explaining some things to him and I needed the help in explaining my frustrations about his lack of a job. This marriage was still very new and when you are in the beginning stages of a marriage, you don't want the other person to see your faults. It's very much like when you first start dating, but now he was around all the time. I was used to my house being exactly that....my house. I was used to seeing him on weekend visits and then we would part ways. I was used to him paying his bills and I was used to paying my bills, but now we are together. Now I was the only one working and paying all of the bills.

My husband did not like the idea of therapy. He bucked at it and didn't fully participate like I wished he would have. He didn't speak much at all. He only said a few words here and there and wouldn't look up during the sessions. I begged him to be open to this and that if we truly put forth the effort then things would get better especially in the sex department. And I knew how much he wanted that to improve, but he still didn't feel like he needed to go to therapy with me to help resolve the anxiet-ies I had around that particular area. He felt like it was my problem to fix and that by now there shouldn't be an issue with it. This definitely put a strain on our relationship be-cause I desperately needed his help. I needed to feel secure with him in a monetary fashion as well. I didn't want his parents to keep paying for things, I wanted him to pay for those items. The idea of the man I had married began to change. When we were dating he had a job and paid for things at least that is what I thought. I was supposed to be submissive to him, but he was supposed to help with the bills. This idea that I was supposed to do everything and be submissive and not get upset, was beyond what I could do. The frustration arose and instead of spending more time together we spent more time with my friends parents since we were not that far away. This also created frustration on his part because he felt like we should be spending more time together. But I didn't want to spend that time with him when he was so closed off on therapy and the few times he went, he wasn't open to it at all. It was a hard time in our marriage and our marriage was just starting. We went from the high of the actual wedding to the honeymoon and then the reception to where we were now. Coming from such a pure happiness to the everyday struggles of life was a hard adjustment. It wasn't a change that I dealt with particularly well.

WILL THIS MOVE
BE THE LAST?

MY HUSBAND BEGAN to look for a graduate program which met his needs. Through a long series of interesting events he landed at Stephen F. Austin State University in Nacogdoches, Texas. This meant yet another move. I had to tell my district that I wouldn't be returning the following year but I was able to do summer school. Thankfully they allowed me to work in the summer as this is what paid for everything necessary for the move including the down payment and rent for the apartment we found. Once again I would be moving to a place where I didn't know a single soul. A place far away from anybody I knew. Last time when I moved to Tahlequah, I was still about an hour away from my friends family and even closer to her, but this move would be different. I would be several hours away and would be navigating this marriage on my own. Therapy would also have to stop since I wouldn't be anywhere near my therapist. This wasn't the time for a move. Everything about this move scared me. I knew my husband wouldn't be able to provide much since he would be in school and I would have to find some sort of job that paid enough to cover everything.

Because of a grant I got during my postgraduate I had to do therapy in the schools for two years. Well this would be year two if I could get the job. The interview was intimidating to say the least. The other speech therapists in the district were the ones who interviewed me before the special education director did. I didn't know what I was walking into. I just knew I had to make a good impression several times over. Really once I started talking and answering their questions my nerves subsided but this was kind of my only option as far as a job went. It ended up being a pretty lengthy process and I was interviewed for four hours. About a week later I was notified that I had gotten the job. I was so excited but now I had to figure out the rules and regulations for practicing speech pathology in Texas and let me tell you it is so different than practicing in Oklahoma.

The day came for the big move and there were a lot of moving parts. This was by far my biggest move not only in distance but in the amount of possessions to move. Of course with my moves it was either the coldest day of the year, raining, or the hottest day of the year. There wasn't a single move that I did in which the weather was nice, but that's how it went. And this move just so happened to be on the hottest day of the summer. Lucky us.

I am the person that when I am living in an apartment, I want to be on the top floor so I don't have to hear the people above me. So, the hottest day of the year with a lot more stuff to move and emotions running high didn't equate for a very good time. It was definitely a high stress move.

Once things were settled everyone slowly went their separate ways leaving my husband and I alone. Alone with boxes upon boxes to unpack and organize. I know I shouldn't have felt so alone that first night. I was with my husband afterall, but I felt like everyone I knew and loved besides my husband had just walked out of my life. I had grown very accustomed to being back with my friends family over the past year or so and had gotten very close to them once again. So now it felt like it did in Tahlequah when they walked out and didn't know if they would ever come to visit.

OUR NEW LIFE

OUR APARTMENT SLOWLY began to take shape as boxes were unloaded and we began to settle into a new normal. Nacogdoches was different in many ways that what I had previously been used to. For one the in-town speed limit was much higher. There was a university in town but for once I wasn't attending that university. We were in Texas were there doesn't seem to be much of a season change. Just winter, pollen, and summer. Texas in regards to my professional paperwork was very different than what I knew. Different than what I had studied. Some of the terminology was the same, but the definitions were different. What I once felt confident doing, I now felt completely out of sorts. I spent a lot of time at home trying to figure out this paperwork and the different regulations in Texas all while trying to navigate a new marriage away from everyone I knew. It was a challenging time, but I was also so happy to be married to my husband.

Soon enough school began for both of us. It was a new and exciting time but also pretty nerve racking. I wasn't quite ready for this reality, but here it was. My husband didn't have to go into school until after I had already left for the day, but he got up with me every morning. He would make my coffee and walk me to my car. He would also randomly leave notes in my car or in my lunch. Oh it was wonderful being in love. He would kiss me goodbye and would text me throughout the day. I knew he loved me and man oh man did I love him. When we were both home at night we would cuddle together on the couch and watch tv or I would watch him play one of his video games. We both shared a love of books and were often caught sitting and reading together. We had a lovely balcony which we decorated and enjoyed together. We were away from everyone we knew which forced us to work on our relationship. I loved coming home at night knowing my husband was there. Knowing I would get to spend the evening with someone I deeply loved. I looked forward to coming home.

As life continued and we settled into our new normal things didn't always come so easily. I wanted to desperately please my husband. I very much wanted to make my friends family proud of me. I wanted to prove to myself that I wasn't who my parents said I was. I wanted to prove them wrong. I wanted to be perfect in every sort of way.

When things became harder, I put more pressure on

myself. My husband became busier and busier with school and we wouldn't get to spend as much time together anymore. Our relationship slowly dwindled while his school relationships blossomed. It came to a point where if I wanted to see my husband, I would have to go to his office at school to do so. I couldn't understand why he couldn't make time to be with me. I knew that his schooling was important but I didn't realize it was going to completely overtake our relationship. And it wasn't just that he was busy, but that there literally wasn't any time for me in his new world. I could see pockets of time where we could spend time together but those pockets were always filled with something else he wanted to do. This in turn put more pressure on me. I figured he wasn't happy with me or the marriage since he didn't want to spend any time with me anymore. It became very hard for me knowing our love for each other was so very different.

I knew things weren't great but I was doing my absolute best to make him happy. I knew that he craved the intimacy I just wasn't yet able to provide. It wasn't that I didn't want to be close to my husband in that capacity, it was just that I hadn't worked through my trauma in that particular area. I tried everything under the sun, but the majority of the time I went back to the trauma with my brother. I went back to this area that I couldn't recover from. I had worked up the courage to ask my husband for some help and there were things I needed from him. The conversation was hard and uncomfortable but I left that conversation feeling good. He had happily agreed to help in any sort of way. He longed for the intimacy but also agreed to take things at my pace and said he wanted me to be comfortable.

Now you have to remember that girl best friends talk about everything and this was no exception. She knew about my past and the struggles I was currently having. I even talked to her mom about it so that I could get some advice on what to do. None of these were easy conversations but they were necessary. I longed to make my husband happy in every area and I knew I was the one holding us up in this particular area. I needed help. I needed people who didn't have that kind of background to help me navigate these waters and help me find a different point of view on sex. I relied on them. Each time that I talked to them the conversation boiled down to a couple of things. 1. I needed to get over it. 2. I was to be submissive to my husband in all areas. 3. I was physically, emotionally, and mentally hurting him by not giving him what he needs. With each phone call my heart broke a little more. They believed I was purposefully withholding from my husband. They believed that I was sinning by not giving him what he wanted. I couldn't control the flashbacks any more than they could control blinking. I was trying my best to be submissive but I just couldn't.

With each failed attempt I felt worse and worse about myself. My husband also became increasingly mad. I was stuck in this vicious cycle that I couldn't get out of. I couldn't change what happened to me, but I also couldn't change the flashbacks. I couldn't change the way I reacted and felt toward sex. My friends family couldn't see that I was trying my best. Maybe it was the distance or maybe they thought tough love was the way to go. I desperately wanted to make everyone happy but I was failing horribly. My friend told me that if I didn't get over it and give my husband what he wanted he would go get it somewhere else. It was statements like these that pulled me further and further into depression. It was these statements that only made things worse. I was full of shame. As a wife I am to provide these things for my husband and I couldn't do it. Because I couldn't do it, it meant I was failing as being a wife. I felt despicable in his eyes. He began to change more into someone I didn't recognize. He became more controlling. He wanted to know where I was at all times. My husband who I loved so deeply would spend hours by himself in the bathroom with the door locked. When he could have been spending time with me, he chose to either be at school behind a locked door or be at home behind a locked door.

I tried to talk to my friend and her family but my feelings and what was going on just didn't translate well on the phone. I wanted them here to witness this behavior. Or here so he would stop this behavior during that time at least. When I called I consistently became discouraged. All of our marital issues were blamed on me. Regardless of how I felt or what I needed, I was to somehow put all of that aside and give him what he wanted. Him not talking to me became my fault. Him locking himself behind doors was my fault. Him not spending time with me was my fault. Everything that was wrong, was my fault. With each phone call or text, it was pounded into me that I was the one to blame. With time, I just couldn't handle it anymore. I couldn't handle the stress at work, at home and with my friend and her family. Something had to go, so the texting and the calling greatly decreased. I couldn't handle being told that everything was always my fault and that my needs or feelings didn't matter.

I was at a loss. I had finally found a therapist in town and started going to her regularly. She was so good for helping me work through so much, but anybody with trauma will tell you, the work is never finished. As soon as you take a few steps forward, a whole 'nother wave of work hits you like ton of bricks. Therapy is a process. It's a slow process. It's a hard process. It's a necessary process. So even though I was going to therapy again, it didn't mean all my troubles stopped.

I wanted my husband. I wanted the man I fell head over heels in love with to come back to me. I wanted to know what I had done so incredibly wrong. He became more demanding about what was for dinner and how it needed to be made. He became more controlling with his personal items. He wouldn't allow me to touch his phone or his computer. He became mad if I wanted to watch tv rather than watch him play his video games. He became mad if things weren't done the way he wanted them done. He became mad if I asked for his help in cleaning or putting his clothes in the hamper. He became mad if I didn't wake up when he woke up. He became mad and I became scared. I could see the turn in his eyes. I could hear the change in his tone. I could see the temper strewn body movements. I did everything I could to see the twinkle of love in his eyes. To see that beautiful smile come across his face. I did everything possible to see his shoulders relax and for his tone to become loving and playful. I lived for these moments. These moments were absolutely glorious. It was like I fell in love with him all over again in these moments. Each moment created this new wave of love which kept me in this cycle.

CYCLE SHIFT

I HATED THE cycle. I just wanted to stomp on the breaks and make it stop. But man I fell in love with this guy. It didn't take long before I felt like a complete fool. See during this time, I found out that his family always paid for everything for him. His car, his schooling, his rent, his food, his clothes, etc. The money he made, well that was some play money. So the little bit that he made with his job at the school became his play money and his alone. The money I made, had to pay for the rent, utilities, my car payment, food, eating out together, dates, etc. I never once saw the money he made. I turned into the biggest fool. I had fallen so in love and I thought he had fallen in love with me. I began to find out, he had loved that I was successful and that I could pay for his things. I had fallen in love and looked for signs. I asked my friend and her family to look for signs. But I didn't find any and neither did they. So now that everything was falling apart, I became the fool in all of their eyes. Just like before, they all thought I was crying wolf. I was once again completely and utterly alone.

I could handle being a disappointment to everyone. I could handle the yelling. I couldn't handle the physical abuse. I couldn't go through this again. I had finally gotten out of the previous abuse. I had severed the relationship with my biological family. I had completely stopped talking to them. They didn't know where I was. They didn't even know I was married. My ties to them were completely cut. Oh I still had plenty to work through, but I wasn't having to live in their drama anymore. It had taken so long for me to get out of that abuse only to end up right back in it.

I realized that if I was right back into the abuse then it must mean that I truly was meant to be abused That it was all of my fault. That I was the one to blame. I believed that I really was no good. I believed that everything my parents had said about me was true. I believed that I was stuck. I believed the words of my friend when she said I could never stand on my own two feet. I believed my friend when I was told that I make things up and that they couldn't possibly be true. I believed my parents words when they said that I only got what I deserved. I believed their words when they said I wasn't good for anything. I believed I was a complete failure. I believed their words that I was the one sinning in this marriage and that I was at fault. I believed my husband's words when he said that if I would just have sex with him he wouldn't get so mad. I believed my husband's words when he said that if I would quit doing things on purpose he wouldn't get so upset. I believed my husband when he said he was sorry and that he would never do it again. I believed my husband when he said that we could take things slow. I believed my husband when he said how much he loved me. I believed my husband's words in each and every note he wrote.

The cycle didn't stop. I wasn't able to get out of it. I wasn't able to put the brakes on. The person I had become was going away. I wasn't happy anymore. I wasn't outgoing. I was tired of putting a show on with my husband at church and with his friends. I was tired of living a double life. I was tired of the name calling. I was tired of failing at everything I did. I was tired of being a failure. The abuse continued on regardless of what I did. I was so completely helpless. There was a change in me that everyone could see. I couldn't cover it up anymore. I didn't tell them what was going on, but I couldn't change how I carried myself. I couldn't change how somber my face looked. I couldn't change the amount of anxiety I was feeling. I couldn't get out from under the deep heavy blanket of depression. I had sworn to myself that I wasn't going to be anything like my biological family. I had sworn no man was going to physically hurt me again, but here I was and it was happening over and over again. My life was a mess. I went from such a happy human being to a very dismal one. My life had drastically changed.

Maybe A New Connection

WHILE AT WORK I had to work very closely with the special education teachers. Because of the sheer number of students we wouldn't just talk every so often. We had to talk multiple times every day. A couple of things occur when this happens. 1.You can develop a great working relationship and that is it. 2.You can develop an annoyance for having to work so closely but do it anyway because that is what your students need. 3.You develop a great working relationship and become friends. For me #3 is what happened. There were so many students at the school I was currently working at that many times I would end up within the resource classroom almost every 30 minutes. I was in and out of there all day long. It sure did help to ensure I got my steps in. Because I was in that classroom so often because we shared so many students, this wonderful teacher became a friend. Now by friend, I mean a very shallow friend at this time. I was a little gun shy on the whole friendship thing and my husband was so controlling now that I didn't want him to find out somehow. For me it was a very superficial level type of friendship, but for her it seemed different. It was much easier for her to open up and tell me some things about herself. For her it all came out so naturally much like blinking.

Our working relationship continued to grow. We ended up spending a lot of time together within the working hours between the kids, meetings and brainstorming different techniques. With time I began to feel more comfortable around her. I began to see myself smile and not feel as if I had to fake everything. I slowly began to feel more like myself around her. And a little glimmer of light creeped its way back into my life.

FRIENDSHIP

I HAD FELT isolated at church because my husband was adamant that nobody know about our marital issues. I felt very isolated at work. I couldn't seem to get the paperwork right. As soon as I thought I had it down, it would change. I felt lonely since I was told repeatedly that everything was my fault. I would wake up and just walk through the motions filled with anxiety with each step that I took. My friendship continued to blossom with Faith as the days passed. I was miserable at home and was fearful of my husband. But with Faith, I felt more relaxed. As with any friendship that grows, you begin to ask questions about one another. I never really knew how to answer these. Do I be truthful and take the chance or do I go with what people want to hear? It was a constant conundrum. I decided to take a chance with Faith. I didn't say much but I said enough to where I felt like I had said too much. But she didn't run away. She didn't think that I was too much and was just going to be trouble. She stayed and we kept talking. I don't know if her opinion of me changed that day, but I know my opinion of her changed. *If I can say that and she doesn't run away, this may be the answer to my prayers.* I began to slowly open up more and more with Faith. She was starting to find out things about me that no one really knew. I began to tell her that my husband and I were having issues. She didn't know the extent and she didn't know about the abuse, but knew we were having problems. She didn't tell me that everything was my fault and that it was up to me to fix it. She encouraged me to do little things and not worry about the big things that were so hard for me.

NEW PLAN

I STARTED TO spend more time with Faith and her ever changing kids. I loved watching them interact with one another and how easily motherhood came to Faith. I desperately wanted that. I so wanted to be a good mom and prove everyone wrong. I was going to love my kids probably too much. I was going to shower them with unending raindrops of love. We were going to go on picnics. We were going to go camping and roast marshmallows. We were going to go on vacations and bear hunts. We were going to spend lots of time outside playing and getting dirty. We were going to learn how to throw and catch a ball. I was going to be the magazine mom. I was going to be everything that my mom wasn't. I wasn't ever going to yell at my kids. I wasn't ever going to be mean to them. I wasn't ever going to tell them to "go away" or "because

I said so". Oh the more I was with Faith and those little ones, the more baby fever came over me. I wanted to hold and nurture my baby. I wanted to get pregnant. The man I fell in love with would have been such a good father and I knew if I could just get over sex and get pregnant then everything would be okay. Our problems would fade because we would have this precious being to take care of. My husband and I talked about kids several times. He wanted kids and so did I. He really wanted kids when he was done with school and I really wanted kids now. I was convinced that if I got pregnant then I could prove to my friend and her family that see, we did have sex. I could prove to them that I was making my husband happy and that not everything was my fault. I could prove to myself that I wasn't such a failure and could finally be good at something.

I began to buy little books and peruse the card section looking for the perfect card to tell my husband I was pregnant. I would daydream of how I would tell him and how different our lives would be. I would daydream about how loving of a father he would be and how much he would love me for giving him this precious gift. This idea allowed me to deal with everything else. To deal with the stress at work. To deal with the stress of my friend and her family. And to deal with the stress with my husband.

It was a guiding hope. A guiding hope that faded. God should have been my guide and my hope but I wasn't feeling very particularly fond of him these days. I thought people at church could help our marriage. I thought they could give us some advice or at least tell us that they have gone through some similar struggles. But my husband wouldn't allow it. And I was too fearful to speak. As the abuse became more frequent, parts of me were dying quickly. I was forming into what he wanted, but that didn't stop the abuse. He still wasn't happy. His words were just words. He would say that he loved me but wouldn't show that. He would say that he wouldn't do it again, to do it just a few hours later.

THE TURNING POINT

I WOULD TELL Faith that I just simply couldn't touch him anymore. That it was too hard. I couldn't sit near him and sleeping in the same bed with him was next to impossible. I was breaking and I was breaking hard. Everything I had worked so hard for was dying away. Each moment I lost another part of me.

I began to spend hours with Faith. I figured it didn't matter anyway since my husband wasn't home often and when he was, I was getting hit or choked or thrown or pinned down. I didn't want to be there but I also didn't see a way out, so I would spend hours with Faith. I wouldn't go back to my apartment until 2 or 3AM. Faith and I would talk but most importantly she would let me sleep. Sleep wasn't happening but for maybe an hour or two a night. The flashbacks were in full force. They happened at night and during the day. I was in a constant fight or flight mode. My body never relaxed. I needed somewhere safe. I needed someone who could see that not everything was my fault. I needed my friend and her family, but there wasn't much encouragement happening. I didn't need to be beat down, I needed someone to see me where I was and help me.

One night Faith said the most precious words I could have ever heard. "You can always come here. This is a safe place. You are loved. You are important. You are safe. My house is always open day or night." I knew she meant them too. That it wasn't just somebody saying what they think you want to hear, but she truly meant it. I knew I could go to her house. I knew I would be safe there. The prayer for safety had been answered. Not in the way I wanted, but it had been answered. See I wanted my home to be safe. I wanted to feel safe at my home, but that safety just wasn't there. That safety was with Faith and in her home.

Seeing Is Believing

MY HUSBAND AND I were still together on a chilling night in October. The high school bands in this area put on a marching competition at the university. Since my husband and I were both band nerds, we had to go. We were looking forward to it and it was a date that didn't cost anything. I told him I had told Faith's kids that we would sit with them and look at all of the instruments. So when we got there we found them and made ourselves comfortable. As the night progressed I became chilly. I was wearing a hoodie and went to put my jacket on. Well I obviously have issues with items being tight on my neck so I asked my husband to fix the hood on the hoodie and pull it out so it was laying on top of the jacket. At this point Faith knew a little bit about the abuse so she was watching interactions very closely.

I was sitting in front of him and he grabbed the hood of the hoodie. All was good. He was in a good mood. We were being huge band nerds and the kids were enjoying every second of it. He then grabbed the hood and began to pull backwards while putting his knees in my back and pushing me forward as the hood was choking me. I felt a wave of panic rush over me. *We are in public! There are kids right here! Let go, Let Go, LET GO!!!!!!!!!* Faith had seen it and was shocked that this was happening. It felt like he was choking me for an eternity, but it was probably only a few seconds when all was said and done. I figured the rules were different since we were in public so I was going to say something. I said something to the effect of asking hm why he did that when all I asked was to put the hood on my jacket. His response will be one that I will never forget and I don't think it will be one that Faith will forget. He said, "Well I gotta have some fun."

What Just Happened

It was a Sunday afternoon and my husband was on his soapbox about something. He was getting more and more mad with each syllable he said. He was yelling at me for this and for that and was coming at me quickly. My biological family conditioned me to just take the abuse. To not run because if you ran then you got it so much worse. They conditioned me to just stand there or lay there or sit there or whatever position. I wasn't to move and I wasn't to make noise. When you grow up like this, that is your automatic response. So here my husband is with rage filled eyes, screaming about God knows what, and stomping towards me. And here I was standing still like I am supposed to. This was the most violent he had gotten with me. This was the most hitting and grabbing and pushing and pulling he had done. And I was at my wits end. I don't know if I packed a bag. I don't know if I walked down the hall-way to get my school stuff. I just remember showing up at Faith's door with tears streaming down my face. My hair was all over and I was crying so hard I was barely standing up. I ran. I ran to the only place I could. I ran to where it was safe. I ran.

When I finally stopped crying I couldn't believe what I had done. I couldn't believe what he had done. And I couldn't believe that I was going to be stuck in this abusive marriage for the rest of my life. I so desperately wanted to tell my friend, but I knew she wouldn't believe me. She hadn't believed anything else I was saying. She just be-lieved I was to blame. I knew I couldn't handle her dis-comforting words so I just avoided her and her family.

One day with Faith turned into a week, and then 2 weeks, and then a couple of months. I couldn't go back to my husband. But I also couldn't get divorced. You see I grew up with it being preached that if I got a divorce, I was going to Hell. I grew up with divorce being the un-pardonable sin. I knew my friend and her family would never in a million years approve of a divorce and I was afraid I would lose them for good if I got divorced. But I couldn't be abused for the rest of my life. I couldn't go back to that life. Something had to give. I was stuck be-tween two choices which were unthinkable. They weren't possible. The only possible choice I had was to stay with Faith in her home. That was the only good choice I could have made.

While I was living with Faith I was still paying all of

the bills for my husband. I had this insane notion that with me being gone for a little bit then he would change. Then he would treat me better. Then he would be the man I fell in love with. That he wouldn't have girls behind locked doors. That he wouldn't be so controlling. I had this belief that things were going to get better, so I still paid for everything. I had asked him several times to go to therapy with me. That we could get some help and we could work this out. But I told him I was not coming back until he and I had gone to therapy and worked through some things. I told him I was not going to come back to the abuse. He would say that he would go to therapy after I moved back in with him, but my trust had been completely and utterly broken. I needed to see improvement before I was alone with him in that apartment. I begged. I pleaded. I wrote him letters. I called him. Faith had him over at the house so we could talk, but still things didn't change. He was only worried about his schooling and how difficult it would be if he took a year off to work on our marriage. He would say that I didn't love him by asking him to put his schooling on hold for a year. The conversations were hard and there were lots of tears shed by both him and me.

Things weren't getting better but I needed my friend and her family. I needed their support, not their judgement. I needed them to understand what was going on. They had accepted my husband into their family. My friend saw him as a brother and they were close. I knew it was going to be a loss for them if we divorced. I was very nervous to tell them because I was so fearful of their reaction. The last time we had talked they were so adamant that things were my fault and that I needed to fix them. And here I was telling them that I couldn't fix it. That it was broken beyond repair. They felt like I had deceived them and betrayed them by not telling them everything that was happening. The sad part of all of this, is that I had told them several times on the phone, but yet they never once believed me. They told me I betrayed them by not telling them that I had moved out. My friend said I went and found somebody who was going to feel sorry for me and believe all of my lies. She said that as soon as things started to get hard I ran away. She said that I never wanted to get married and I shouldn't have because now I have hurt an awesome guy. She was mad that she wasn't going to see him at family functions anymore. They said that it was wrong of me to move in with Faith and that I made a vow to God regarding my marriage. They said there was no way I could raise kids especially foster kids. She said, I can't even stand on my own two legs much less teach someone right from wrong. She said I was sinning by moving in with a lady and flat out asked me if I was a lesbian now. (Side note: I do not have any issues with gay, lesbian, etc. You love who you love. It's not my business and who am I to say how you can or can't love.) I told them I was not a lesbian but I ran to a safe place. I desperately needed somewhere safe that wouldn't keep telling me that everything was my fault. My friend got very upset with Faith and I working together as foster parents to these children. My friend would continually say that I was damaging the kids because all I do is damage everything. She said I was confusing the kids by there being two women in the house. I was told that I am the one who failed the marriage because I ran out. I was told that I needed to fix it and if he wouldn't talk to me too bad, it was still my job to fix it. I was told that my feelings and needs didn't matter. I was told that I was making everything up. The final straw was when I was told that my friend and her family would not support me and would no longer support me in anything if I got divorced.

I realized then, that their love was truly conditional. They could only love me if I fell in line with them every single time. They could only love me if I abided by their rules. They couldn't love someone who had gotten a divorce. They couldn't love someone who they saw as a liar. They couldn't believe what was going on because they liked my husband so much. They loved him so much that they looked past every single fault and solely placed the blame on me.

DARK

OH THAT DEPRESSION was dark. I stopped eating. I stopped getting out of bed. I stopped getting dressed. Faith had to physically get me out of bed to go to work. I never smiled. I cried all the time. I didn't want to live anymore. I fell so uncontrollably in love and everything frantically fell apart. I was worthless. I was a failure. Everything I had done to prove my biological family wrong, hadn't happened. I was the problem. It was all my fault.

My husband and I had stopped talking until one day when he called to tell me I had to get everything out by the next morning. I immediately burst into tears. He couldn't afford the apartment and I had emptied the bank account. It was my last ditch effort and it ended up just pushing him farther away. By this time I had already been talking to some people at church because they noticed he wasn't coming anymore. He also wouldn't answer any of their phone calls. I needed all the help I could get to get my stuff out of the apartment. There was a whole team that met me there. They saw me frantic and sobbing. Faith helped me be able to get through the process and deciding what to keep and what not to keep. I was fortunate enough to have a storage building where my stuff lived for many months. They helped a horrible situation go as smoothly as it possibly could. They wrapped me in hugs when I was overcome with grief and made sure everything was gone. I couldn't thank them enough.

I asked them all to wait in their cars while I stayed in the apartment. I know that this goodbye was final. It was saying goodbye to the dream of having a marriage like Grace's. It was saying goodbye to the dream of being a mom like Grace and Faith. It was saying goodbye to my husband and the good memories within those walls. It was saying goodbye to my friend and her family. Yes it was just an apartment, but it was saying goodbye to everything I had worked so hard for. I was overwhelmed with sadness. It was the keeling over, clutching your stomach, loud screaming sobs. Everything was gone. All hope had vanished. I had lost my husband, my best friend, and the family I had prayed so long and hard for all at the same time. What made it worse was that they were still alive and choosing to walk away. I think in many ways it would have been easier if they had all died because then I would feel like the trash they could throw to the curb and never look at again.

Everything was gone. I couldn't bear to see my items that my husband and I shared but I also couldn't bear to get rid of them. The depression just continued to wash over me and beat me down. The world didn't stop just because my world had turned upside down. There were kids in the house and I had to find some way to get out of bed at least once a day. It took an extremely long amount of time but getting out of bed became easier bit by bit.

Starting New

Then this set of kids came into the house and they were not cute. I hadn't ever seen foster kids come into a house before. I had never seen what they looked like after they have been pulled from their parents. They didn't have anything except for what they were wearing. They were scraggly and needed some baths. I didn't know what I was supposed to do. Faith was talking to the people that brought the kids and signing paperwork and here I was staring at the kids. I didn't know if I should touch them or call them by their names. I didn't know if I was supposed to play with them. I was so outside of my element. Faith just scooped them up and started loving on them. Telling them her name and getting toys for them to play with. *Oh, that's what I'm supposed to do.* Oh but man those scraggly kids began to tug on my heart. They made me get out of bed. They made me learn how to teach them how to play. They made me make new traditions and break out of my depressive shell. They taught me how to love and forgive. They taught me that love truly can heal a person. Those not so cute kids became the most beautiful children I have ever seen. Oh how I loved them. I loved teaching them words and how to talk. I loved playing in the yard with them. I loved our tea parties and seeing their eyes light up when they experienced something for the first time. I began to get a twinkle in my eye. I began to enjoy life. I began to become that mother Grace showed me. I began to become that mother Faith showed me how to be. Faith helped me navigate these waters. And I learned how wrong I was about motherhood. I was going to get upset with my kids. I was going to talk in a harsh tone every so often. I was going to say, "because I said so." But I wasn't going to beat them. I wasn't going to hurt them. I showered those raindrops of love on them and they showered raindrops of love on me. Then their baby brother came to us. The siblings were together. Faith had to teach me everything regarding a baby. Yes I had babysat before and yes I had worked at a daycare who accepted kids at 15 months. I didn't know what to do with a baby. I cherished rocking him and singing to him at night. I cherished watching him learn how to roll over and crawl. I treasured watching his siblings interact with him. These three kids filled the canyon size hole I had. They gave me a family. They gave me a purpose. They gave me a sense of belonging and pulled me out of my deep dark depression. Those three changed my life. They changed my life in ways they don't know. They changed the entire outlook of my life.

Those three were the first group of kids I had seen come into foster care and exit. A most wonderful, glorious, beautiful family adopted them. It could have only been a match made by God himself. There was an instant connection. The kids would be adopted together and have a forever family. It was the most beautiful thing I have ever seen. And selfishly it was the most heartbreaking loss I had ever experienced. I had become so completely attached to those kids. They were the best thing that had ever happened and now I had to say goodbye. I had to choose to let them go because I knew it was what was best for them. I never understood a love so strong that it hurt, but I totally understand it now. Those three kids in many ways showed me how to be a mom. Selfishly I miss them deeply, but I am filled with such happiness knowing that they have their forever family.

I haven't looked back since those three. Foster care is devastatingly hard and extraordinarily rewarding. Many say they couldn't do it. That they would get too attached. Believe me, I get attached. I get too attached, but that attachment means that they know love. That they have experienced love. That they have felt safe and secure. That attachment means everything to them and to me. Each and every day, these kids make my life complete. Every day I get to look perseverance in the eye. It may be in a 4-year-old girl or a 10-year-old boy. I get to see optimism in the eyes of 3-year-old boys and 7-year-old girls. I get to see their strength as the overcome hurdles both literally and figuratively. I get to see them develop a sense of confidence and self-worth. I get to hear their precious prayers and their songs about God. I get to see the gentleness of God every day. I have the honor of telling them about God and showing them God's love. I have the pleasure of seeing them experience things for the first time. I get to be the mom I dreamt of being. I get the chance to see how much these kids change. And with each kid, I grow and change. Every day I am reminded of how far I have come and feel so blessed that Faith took a chance on me. They may be with me for a couple of days to years, but with each one tears are shed from my eyes but I wouldn't change it for the world.

God had a plan all along, I just didn't see it. Because of my past, I am in the unique position to know firsthand how these kids might be feeling. But my past is not my present. My past does not define me. My past simply allows me to know exactly what not to be. And each and every day, I am thankful that I made it through everything so that I could make a small difference in this world.

There was a time in my youth where I so greatly needed a safe place and no one was there. There was a time in my adulthood where I so greatly needed a safe place. I finally found it despite all of the hardships. And I am now that safe place for children that need it.

CPSIA information can be obtained
at www.ICGtesting.com
Printed in the USA
LVHW040813050820
662303LV00002B/210